BOLD Leadership

BOLD Leadership

The Adventure of Building Excuse-Proof, Goal-Crushing Teams

By Kim Svoboda

BOLD Leadership: The Adventure of Building Excuse-Proof, Goal-Crushing Teams

Copyright ©2026 Kim Svoboda

987654321
First Edition
Printed in the United States of America.

Cover design by Jay Elliott and Jake Clark, Pithy Wordsmithery
Interior layout by Sue Murray, Pithy Wordsmithery
Copyediting by Nils Kuehn, Pithy Wordsmithery
Proofreading by Scott Morrow and Katharine Dvorak, Pithy Wordsmithery

ISBN: 979-8-9996737-0-1 (paperback)
ISBN: 979-8-9996737-1-8 (e-book)
ISBN: 979-8-9996737-2-5 (hardcover)

Kim Svoboda
Email: info@aspirationcatalyst.com
Website: www.aspirationcatalyst.com

Library of Congress Control Number: 2025916273

Praise

"*BOLD Leadership* is a powerful call to action for leaders who are ready to break free from busyness and lead with purpose. Kim Svoboda doesn't just offer tips—she equips you with a bold, clear-eyed road map for building vision, trust, and long-term impact. This book is both strategic and deeply human, helping leaders prioritize what matters most and inspire others to follow. If you're serious about leading with intention instead of inertia, this book will show you the way."

> —**Dr. Marshall Goldsmith**, Thinkers50 #1 Executive Coach and *New York Times* Best-Selling Author of *The Earned Life*, *Triggers*, and *What Got You Here Won't Get You There*

"In *BOLD Leadership*, Kim Svoboda openly shares her personal journey of self-discovery, drawing on challenging experiences that ignited her own leadership transformation. Weaving her discoveries into a memorable framework, Kim tells inspiring real-life stories, reveals hard-won lessons, and offers practical strategies that you can implement immediately. Whether you are at the beginning of your leadership journey or looking to refine your skills, Kim's wisdom and courage provide encouragement and guidance to help you embrace your own leadership adventures. Dive in and discover the bold leader within you!"

> —**James Kouzes**, coauthor of the best-selling *The Leadership Challenge*

"It is with great pleasure and honor that I endorse Kim and her book, *BOLD Leadership*. Kim joined my company in 1991 as a young college graduate and entry-level salesperson. She almost immediately distinguished herself and quickly grew into a leadership role, inspiring and leading a new division and team. If I were still at the company, I would never have let her leave. She has since gone on to accomplish great things—building, leading, and inspiring. Even I, an old dog, can and do continue to learn from her."

> —**Michael P. Krasny**, Founder, Former CEO & Chairman Emeritus of CDW, and Current President, Sawdust Investment Management Corporation

"Having known Kim Svoboda for over twenty years, I've witnessed firsthand her unwavering integrity and unique ability to empower those around her. In this remarkable book, she illuminates the BOLD framework—brilliant vision, one-ness, lighthouse leadership, and daring drive—with clarity and authenticity. Through vivid storytelling and actionable insights, Kim offers a profound road map for those ready to step up and make a lasting impact. Her two decades of leadership experience and coaching mastery shine through in every page, making this book an essential guide for leaders who dare to be bold—and the world is better for it."

—**Ana Claudia Dutra**, Chief Executive Officer of Mandala Global Advisors, Inc., & Global 8x Board Director

"I enthusiastically endorse Kim Svoboda—her coaching has sharpened our leadership focus and elevated performance across every level of our organization. In *BOLD Leadership*, she distills those transformative insights into an inspiring, actionable guide; even the opening chapter challenges leaders to dream bigger and execute with conviction."

—**Jerry Weidmann**, CEO, Wolter Group, LLC

"For years, Kim has helped our high performers grow into bold, effective leaders. Now she's captured that approach in *BOLD Leadership*. This book is filled with the practical strategies and mindset shifts that make a real difference in leadership today."

—**Matt Massucci**, CEO, Hirewell

"*BOLD Leadership* is more than a leadership book—it's a rallying cry for courageous, results-driven leadership. Kim Svoboda delivers a clear, strengths-based framework and practical tools that help leaders move from vision to measurable success, all while leading with heart, purpose, and conviction."

—**Margaret Mueller**, Managing Director and Chief Growth Officer, Tilia Holdings, Inc., and Former CEO of Executives' Club of Chicago

"Kim has been a force multiplier for our leadership team—her bold approach challenged us to think bigger, communicate with clarity, and lead with intent. *BOLD Leadership* distills her proven strategies into a must-read for any executive looking to scale both performance and purpose. Highly recommended."

—**Ian Kieninger**, CEO, Avant Communications

"*BOLD Leadership* is a practical and inspiring guide for anyone ready to lead with courage, clarity, and purpose. I'm proud to champion this important work and honored to be part of its journey."

—**Rosemary Swierk**, President, Direct Steel, LLC

"A brilliant vision isn't just about seeing the future—it's about believing in one bold enough to change everything. This book is your invitation to dream bigger, lead braver, and ignite a movement that matters."

—**Jon Harris**, EVP, Chief Communications and Networking Officer, Conagra Brands

"Kim Svoboda masterfully blends heart, authenticity, and performance to guide leaders who want to elevate themselves and the world around them. *BOLD Leadership* inspires leaders to step fully into who they are and create meaningful change. This book is a must-read for EVERY leader!"

—**Dorri McWhorter**, President and CEO, Executives' Club of Chicago, and Former CEO of YWCA and YMCA of Metropolitan Chicago

"Kim is a dynamic leader with extensive experience building teams across industries and with visionary leaders. Her vision, passion and drive enables leaders and teams to create a collaborative path forward and a roadmap to achieving objectives and exceeding expectations!"

—**Harry Harczak**, Independent Venture Capital & Private Equity Professional

For Jared, Lilli, and Isabella—
You are the why behind every bold step I take.
Thank you for your love, your laughter, your sacrifices,
and your strength.
This book—and this journey—would not exist without you.
May you always know how much you are loved and how
powerful your presence is in this world.

Table of Contents

"The most common way people give up their power is by thinking they don't have any."
—Alice Walker,
Author of *The Color Purple*

Introduction

Leaders aren't born; they're grown and developed through experience, intentional effort, and continuous learning. Whether they lead well or poorly, leaders create a ripple effect that impacts teams, organizations, and communities far beyond their immediate reach. To lead effectively—and BOLDly—leaders need knowledge, tools, and the necessary skills. Yet many are never offered any sort of leadership training. We expect them to excel, but how can they when they don't know how?

This reminds me of a favorite quote from Maya Angelou: "Do the best you can until you know better. Then, when you know better, do better."

The truth is that many leaders don't realize that there's a gap to close. According to a Gallup poll, 80 percent of leaders rate themselves as above average, but only 20 to 30 percent of their employees agree. The chasm between these perceptions is striking—and costly. Closing this gap requires leaders to elevate their skills, embrace feedback, and commit to growth.

Why do I see leadership as a BOLD adventure? It's simple: I've seen it firsthand. Over the past decade as founder and CEO of Aspiration Catalyst®, I have helped countless leaders crush goals and build high-performing teams. Before that, I spent more than 25 years thriving in corporate America. Through all of it, I have learned that leadership isn't just about showing up; it's about stepping up. Life itself is a grand adventure, and leadership should reflect that same spirit. Leaders hold immense influence. To create a lasting, positive impact, they must be courageous, visionary, and, yes, BOLD.

The inflection point in my journey started like this: I was up for a huge promotion that I was sure I would get. In fact, my boss had assured me that the job was mine. But when it was announced, it wasn't my name that was called. "Disappointed" does not begin to express my emotions in that moment. Then, in what felt like being awarded a sort of consolation prize, I was asked to set up another new division. Although it was an excellent assignment, it was also an enormous undertaking that I was woefully unprepared for. And if I'm being honest, my heart wasn't really in it because my ego was still smarting from the loss of the promotion.

And so it began. Over the next few months, I went through the motions to get the new division up and running. I developed the strategy, created the market approach, built the team, and hired consultants to provide expertise in critical areas. It got pretty complicated quickly as I tried to do too much and please too many people along the way. Soon, I found myself in way over my head.

I was burning the candle at both ends and running myself ragged. I found myself bringing home enormous piles of work every single night—back in the day when people didn't normally do that. I was doing the job of three or more people. It was exhausting, and I didn't feel safe enough to ask for help. I was trying to prove something—to them, to society, to myself.

The role I was in seemed to require a high level of analytical expertise (which was not among my top talents), and I'd signed up for too much way too fast. Instead of prioritizing better, saying no, and finding others to partner with or hire, I kept trying to do it all myself—an approach that didn't work (it never does). The team's continual underperformance was due to my poor leadership. They were lacking direction and facing overwhelming and unreasonable deadlines. There's a saying—you are either winning or explaining—and I ended up spending a lot of time explaining: delays, misses, and failures. And if things weren't bad enough, a colleague with whom I'd always had a contentious relationship suddenly became my direct boss.

IT WAS BLEAK.

I wasn't sure what direction to take to get out of this tremendous hole, but I didn't have to wait long before the direction was provided. I was moved to another division and demoted to a lesser role, leaving me feeling humiliated that I had failed, incredibly unsupported, and alone. I was a failure and a wash-up and had no idea what to do next. I was only 30 years old. Oh, and on top of that, I was also going through a divorce! Needless to say, my life was in a bit of turmoil.

When you're going through one of the worst experiences in your life, it's easier to blame external forces and look for fault in others. The fundamental attribution error wants us to believe this:

If you're achieving, it's because of you. If you're not, it's because of others or outside forces that are out of your control.

BOLD Reflections

As I reflected on this "failure," I knew that, though I was facing some pretty significant external headwinds, all roads led back to what was in my control: namely, my lack of effective leadership. As I pondered the situation, there were several areas that needed some serious attention, and all of them were in my control:

1. A vision for success
2. A strong plan to achieve the vision
3. Authenticity in being true to myself
4. Courage to make decisions and stick to them
5. Confidence to be able to stand my ground and say no
6. Prioritization, not trying to do everything all at once
7. Accountability to drive my performance
8. Humility in admitting what I didn't know and asking for help

In reality, many leaders who are facing times of challenge are dealing with many of the same issues. The only way forward is to be true to yourself. This is a nonnegotiable when it comes to great leadership. When I looked at myself critically in the mirror, I saw that I wasn't fully being true to myself. People pleaser was in the fine print of my LinkedIn profile. It may not have shown on the outside, and I'm guessing some who worked with me at that time would have been surprised to know that I was trying really hard to be what I thought others wanted me to be. The more I went in that direction, the more unsteady I felt. I found myself unable to make decisions, second-guessing and unwilling to admit that I was feeling this way for fear of being found out. I had no idea what to do next and felt paralyzed.

One day, it finally hit me. I had a major case of imposter syndrome. My confidence was shaken, sending me into a destructive cycle of doubt. Who hasn't experienced this? The more I ventured away from my authentic self, the more self-doubt and indecisiveness would creep in. This led to several impacts: avoiding decisions that needed to be made, playing it safe, not taking risks, acting like a jerk with my peers, and not being the inspiring and supportive leader I knew I could be. I was overcome with the fear of failing. I was unable to meet my commitments because I had taken on too much too fast.

You've heard the adage: "When you try to please everyone, you end up pleasing no one." In a nutshell, that was me. I was in a bad place and needed things to change. I looked critically at my situation and took inventory of what was working and what was not. I saw that I needed to stop trying to be the person that others wanted me to be.

I went on a quest to figure out what I needed to do in order to get the train back on the tracks. I spent time discovering what great leadership looks like, along with taking a hard look in the mirror. It was a maturing process and a metamorphosis. Don't get me wrong; I didn't just show up on the mountaintop and all the answers were delivered to me. It was a journey—a long and arduous one. I fought against metamorphosis because it was scary not only in the worst of times but also at the best of times; it was still really, really uncomfortable. Ego, ego, ego—why are you such a pain in the ass?!

"You should do something every day that makes you uncomfortable."

These words sound like a trope delivered by a well-seasoned, revered leader. But think again! They were actually said by none other than my teenage niece Grace, who was sharing this concept with my mom. If this teenager can grasp what the adventure of leadership entails, especially the discomfort that comes along with it, you can too. (And we should definitely keep an eye on Grace, as she's well on her way to becoming an incredibly BOLD leader!)

I dove headfirst into learning all I could about great leadership. I went back to the basics, which coincided with some kick-ass leadership development training I'd received from my new employer. From there, I created a framework of what resonated with me and how I wanted to deliver and be viewed in the world. As I reflected on what had created success along the way, I assembled various components that would eventually lead to developing the BOLD system.

Finally, I discovered one of my favorite game-changing ideas while watching *The Oprah Winfrey Show* one day. Marcus Buckingham was sitting across from her, turning traditional professional development on its head with his eye-opening ideas on leveraging talents and turning them into strengths. He declared, "We are doing it all wrong. We get so focused on what we are doing wrong and spend all our time on things that likely won't improve much." What?! It truly had never occurred to me to invest more in the things I was already good at to make them even stronger.

I, along with many of the leaders we work with, am quick to flip to the back page of the review to look for the negative/critical feedback and spend most of our time, mind space, and effort there. The way I was thinking, my talents were as good as they were going to get, so all my development efforts were focused on improving my weaknesses. But here's what I noticed: the more I worked solely on my weaknesses, the more frustrated I became. The small improvements didn't produce enough ROI (return on investment)—so much time for so little gain. Although I would spend several years in that "desert" trying to improve in the areas I wasn't great in, I also spent time defining leadership and finding myself. After hearing Buckingham's advice, I decided to try it. Sure enough, by investing more into my areas of talent, the more improvement I ultimately experienced!

Next, I introduced this concept to my team and empowered them to leverage their strengths, which is when the lightbulbs started to turn on. Our interactions became a lot more favorable because I focused on their strengths and how they could use them more effectively, instead of trying to fix their weaknesses. I even joked that they could stop avoiding me in the hallway—because with this strengths-based approach, our conversations became much more enjoyable and energizing. Integrating this approach into the BOLD system caused the team's trajectory to change completely. The energy on the team became palpable, and formerly out-of-reach goals suddenly were exceeded. From that point forward, I implemented the talent-led focus of the BOLD system and celebrated as each team member reaped the rewards. These teams were now BOLD, excuse-proof, and goal-crushing.

In my work with leaders, I notice how often they are stuck, prisoners to their own destructive modes of thinking. Deep down, they know that they are destined for something greater, but something holds them back from actually going for it. There seems to be an imaginary rule book they are following that contains constraint after constraint. Usually, these limitations are self-imposed and prevent their BOLDness from coming out—focusing on weaknesses, not having a vision, getting too caught up in the day-to-day, and other modes of operating that simply don't produce BOLD results.

If you're going to embrace what it means to be a BOLD leader, your journey must include entertaining the notion that you can accomplish far more than you ever thought possible. Enlisting your team in achieving BOLDness—inspiring them, motivating them, and paving the way—is the way to achieve greater success.

Every step, even the seemingly small ones, will take you to where you've never been before, and you will reap the rewards. Doing things the same way everyone else does is a recipe for mediocrity.

What Does It Mean to Be a BOLD Leader?

BOLD leadership is an adventure. It has its ups and downs, like a roller coaster. Throughout this book, you will learn about the four elements of BOLD leadership:

- **B**rilliant vision
- **O**neness
- **L**ighthouse leadership
- **D**aring drive

To get yourself into the proper frame of mind, think about what the adventure of leadership is for you. For most, it's taking that road less traveled. There is excitement and wonder that come with the unknown. Paying attention to fear informs planning and enables intentional forward progress. Not having concrete answers is OK, because even when we do, our best-laid plans often end up getting thrown into chaos.

Leaders rarely take the time to construct a road map; however, at the very least, they should always have a vision/goal in mind and work backward from there. They should know what they want to accomplish and envision how it will look and feel when they reach the end destination. Though they may not know what every step on the path required will be to meet those goals and dreams, they should begin to identify the main checkpoints and milestones required. By doing so, they give themselves a certain degree of flexibility because there is always more than one way to reach an end destination, and that's OK.

This framework is a plan that you can follow. But before you begin, you should know that in most leadership journeys, typically nothing goes according to plan. That's why this is a framework and not a *formula*. There is no foolproof method that will take you from point A to point B. The unexpected is pretty much a guarantee and could include any of the following:

- a new competitor taking away business
- a weather disaster such as excessive rain, tornadoes, derecho winds, or hurricanes
- supply-chain issues impacting production and delivery
- difficulties in hiring or retaining, or both
- economic headwinds or volatility in the marketplace
- (less common) a pandemic, tariffs, or fear of recession

In the face of these challenges, many leaders strive to maintain a straight line or stick to the original plan, which doesn't work. BOLD leaders adjust and fine-tune their path in order to continue the momentum of moving forward. When you drive your car on the highway, you don't just hold the steering wheel in a fixed position. If you did, you would veer into oncoming traffic or end up in a ditch. Instead, as you steer the car, you make small adjustments to keep the vehicle on course. Leaders steer in order to respond to the environment, adjust to market conditions, or keep their team on course.

Anyone can hold the helm when the sea is calm.

This framework will enable you to maintain focus even as other forces conspire to deter you from your goal. Every great adventure starts with a significant challenge and a number of obstacles but ultimately ends in a triumph. And who doesn't love a happy ending? There is drama, strife, competition, self-doubt, and never-ending problems, and finally, against all odds, the hero succeeds despite the challenges through pure will, focus, perseverance, and help from a small group of uniquely talented, determined friends.

As you prepare to develop your own path forward to reach your happy ending as a BOLD leader, let's start with a few questions:

- What does success look like in this endeavor?
- What if there were no limits? What would you do? What could you achieve?
- Where is it that you want to go? Why does it matter?
- How will you know when you've made it?
- What is the impact you want to make?
- How do you get from where you are now to where you want to go? What are the major milestones you'll want to achieve along the way?
- Is your goal big enough? Does it inspire and excite you? Does it make you nervous? Does it seem almost out of reach given the resources you currently have but not totally impossible either?

Why This Book?

Why am I writing this book about leadership? Haven't they all been written? What more could be said on this topic? Here's why: our world *desperately* needs great leaders. Look around you. It's not difficult to find leaders who are, frankly, terrible. I've worked for and with a number of them. It's disheartening, annoying, frustrating, demotivating, and soul-sucking. In fact, I'm embarrassed to say that, at times, *I was one of them*—and sometimes, I still am. I strive to improve, and I know you do too, which is why you are reading this book.

BOLDness has always resonated with me. Choosing the road less traveled represents an adventure I have eagerly pursued. Does this sound like you? Or do you wish that it did? This book is designed with you in mind—to inspire and empower you to embrace your journey, enhance your abilities, and lead with clarity and purpose.

It's an invitation to lead BOLDly, creating a ripple effect that transforms your teams and organizations—and the world around you.

My BOLD vision is to empower leaders to discover their true power and potential and leverage their strengths. When leaders take the path of authenticity, they are at their strongest and achieve the most success. In doing so, their belief moves them to BOLD leadership, where they inspire others to do their best work and achieve great success. As we journey together, you'll learn the important elements that make BOLD leadership an effective way to lead and enjoy this exhilarating adventure.

You may not think of yourself as a BOLD leader at this very moment. But if you stay curious and engaged and put my framework into practice, you can make those big, BOLD visions a reality. BOLD leadership will enable you to take the road less traveled—but doing so won't be easy. BOLD leadership will take you to places you haven't been before and likely would have never visited. But the rewards are great and worth all the fear, uncertainty, and doubt.

Still not convinced that this system will work for you? Here's an example of a powerful leader who covers all the bases of BOLD in action.

Dorri McWhorter: A BOLD Leader in Action

Dorri McWhorter doesn't lead with convention—she leads with conviction. Whether transforming the YWCA into a modern social enterprise or stepping into her groundbreaking role as president and CEO of the Executives' Club of Chicago, Dorri brings every element of BOLD leadership to life.

Brilliant Vision

Dorri saw what many others missed: that nonprofits could—and should—run like innovative businesses in order to achieve greater impact. At YWCA Metropolitan Chicago, she's reimagined the 140-year-old organization, expanding services, building strategic partnerships, and even launching an exchange-traded fund (ETF) focused on companies that empowered women. Her vision isn't about incremental progress; it's about systemic transformation.

She lives the truth that vision isn't just what you see—it's what you're willing to build, even when no blueprint exists.

Oneness

Dorri leads with a deep commitment to people, which pulls from her own reflection of who she is and the impact she wants to make in the world, rooted in her deep sense of integrity. In her TED Talks, she challenges leaders to imagine a better future—one built on mutual respect, collaboration, and a shared sense of responsibility. Her leadership isn't about meeting quotas or checking boxes; it's about showing up with courage, care, and character. She brings others into the mission with clarity and conviction, creating space for everyone to contribute and thrive.

Her authenticity and consistency earn trust because she speaks with purpose, listens with intention, and leads with the greater good in mind.

Lighthouse Leadership

In times of uncertainty, Dorri is a steady, illuminating presence. She doesn't just see what's coming; she guides others toward it. She often quotes Buckminster Fuller:

"You never change things by fighting the existing reality. To change something, build a new model that makes the existing model obsolete."

That's exactly what she does—again and again. Whether partnering with tech giants such as Google to close equity gaps or creating business models that generate social value, she shines a light forward and says, "Come with me." And they do.

Daring Drive

Dorri doesn't wait for conditions to improve—she acts to improve them. As the first Black woman in its 110-year history to lead the Executives' Club of Chicago, she has once again stepped into a legacy institution with fresh eyes and fearless energy. She's not maintaining—she's reimagining.

"Doing good is everybody's business," she says—and under her leadership, doing good also gets results.

A Living Example of BOLD

Dorri McWhorter is the embodiment of BOLD leadership:

- She envisions BOLDly.
- She leads with unity and heart.
- She lights the way for others.
- She gets things done.

As you begin this journey into BOLD Leadership, let Dorri's story remind you: the most powerful leaders aren't fixing what is; they're building what's next.

Your Adventure Starts Now

Achieving big things is possible when you lead with vision, authenticity, courage, and follow-through. Like Dorri, don't wait for permission or perfect conditions—build something bold and meaningful from the ground up. That's what BOLD leadership is all about.

You don't have to be a CEO to lead BOLDly. You just have to be willing to see what others can't yet see, act on what matters, and grow into the leader that your team, organization, and community need you to be. This book is your road map. Let's begin the adventure.

SECTION I

Brilliant Vision

Create Your Brilliant Vision

"It was not a vision created from a business plan. It has been an evolution of passion—passion for technology."
—Michael P. Krasny

Brilliance In Vision

Michael Krasny, founder of CDW—the highly successful technology-solutions provider—reminds us that brilliant vision isn't born from rigid planning. It begins with authentic passion, clarity, and the courage to imagine what does not yet exist.

Brilliance is the inspiration behind leadership. It enables the "B" in BOLD. It is the rallying cry to challenge yourself to take your goals to a higher level and inspires everyone around you to do the same. When you look for brilliance in all you do—vision, hiring employees, and doing exemplary work—you raise yourself and others to the highest standard.

When applied to vision, brilliance is lofty yet clear. Climb to the top of the mountain or stand at the edge of the sea. What do you see? If it is a clear day, you can see for miles. The perspective is far, broad, and wide and enables you to take in the whole picture. This view allows you to take your vision, supersize it, and transform it into something brilliant. Dream one size too big so that it feels uncomfortable yet remains attainable.

For a vision to be brilliant, it must be:
- inspiring
- meaningful
- creating value
- impactful
- going beyond the norm

Why does it matter? Brilliant vision enables innovation, experimentation, and optimization to take flight. The most successful companies worldwide have brilliant vision statements that are simple, clear, and easily understood—moving everyone to action. A brilliant vision focuses on the big picture, rewards long-term results, informs key decisions, and ignites collective momentum.

Here are examples of some of our favorite companies and their brilliant vision statements:
- **Apple** – To create the best products on earth, and to leave the world better than we found it.
- **IKEA** – To create a better everyday life for many people.
- **Microsoft** – To help people and businesses throughout the world realize their full potential.
- **Patagonia** – We're in business to save our home planet.
- **Nike** – To bring inspiration and innovation to every athlete in the world.
- **CDW** – To be the leading IT solutions and services provider in the markets we serve.

A brilliant vision beckons us forward. It speaks to a deep yearning within us—the desire to do something truly meaningful. It asks, "What if we actually achieved this? How would it elevate my leadership? How might it reshape our culture in powerful, unexpected ways? What would our stakeholders believe about who we are and what we stand for? How would realizing this vision transform our organization—and what bold new doors would it open next?"

Dream One Size Too Big

There's a constant tension between being bold and being safe. Boldness requires courage—it dares us to dream bigger, take risks, and step into the unknown. Safety, on the other hand, offers predictability and comfort. But comfort rarely leads to transformation. BOLD leaders feel that pull toward safety too—but they choose to walk through fear, not around it. They know that playing it safe might protect the status quo but that it won't ignite change. The real breakthrough comes when you lean into the discomfort of a bigger vision and say, "Even if it's hard, we're doing it anyway."

Whom is this for? Brilliant vision is for everyone: you, your team, and your organization. You can apply this powerful concept wherever you are in your leadership journey. BOLD leaders don't think of their vision as it would be nice if we reached this goal. Instead, they think and say, "We MUST do this! This is our opportunity to achieve big goals and make a meaningful impact—and we will overcome any obstacle that gets in our way."

What Results Would You Rather Achieve?

At Aspiration Catalyst®, we work with CEOs and leadership teams to unlock growth by building bold leaders and high-performing, excuse-proof teams. We believe leadership is the ultimate catalyst for business results, and we've seen time and again that the way leaders show up makes all the difference.

Over the years, we've had the privilege of partnering with organizations across industries—helping them sharpen their vision, align their teams, and elevate their performance. Some leaders lean into control, focusing on minimizing risk and managing what's immediately in front of them. Others embrace vision, casting bold strategies and inspiring their people to rally behind a shared future. Both approaches leave an imprint, but the results could not be more different.

We've seen companies stall under cautious, risk-averse leadership, achieving only incremental gains. And we've also witnessed organizations soar under leaders who are willing to think bigger, challenge limits, and move with courage. The truth is simple: **leadership style doesn't just influence outcomes—it determines them.**

Not all leaders are built the same—and that's a good thing. Different stages of an organization call for different types of leadership. At

CDW, I had a front-row seat to how two CEOs with distinct strengths guided the company through very different eras.

When Michael Krasny founded and led CDW, the company was in an entrepreneurial, build-and-scale phase. His visionary, risk-embracing style fueled extraordinary expansion. Growth soared—sometimes in the double or even triple digits—with a CAGR of roughly 33% per year. His leadership matched that moment in the company's evolution: bold, fast-moving, and innovation driven. The Circle of Service with laser-like focus on the customer combined with incented and empowered coworkers to provide great level of service proved to be a business model built to last.

When the next CEO, John Edwardson, stepped in, the landscape had shifted. CDW was a much larger organization with new expectations from investors, analysts, and a changing marketplace. John was an outward-facing CEO with strong credibility and highly skilled at working with the investor shareholder community—an important capability for where the company was heading. The leadership style naturally evolved. Decision-making became more measured. Risk-taking became more intentional. The focus increasingly shifted toward profitability and operational discipline. The company's CAGR settled to about 12.7% per year, reflecting both the new priorities and the realities of leading a large, maturing business.

At one leadership meeting, John posed a thought-provoking question:

"If you had to choose, would you rather be the best in customer loyalty or the best in high profitability?"

He asked for a show of hands.

"Customer loyalty?" A few hands went up.

"High profitability?" Nearly every hand in the room—including mine—rose.

In the moment, the question felt philosophical. What many of us didn't appreciate was how powerfully a shift in emphasis can ripple through a company. When profitability becomes the primary lens, even unintentionally, customer focus can start to fade from view. We assumed loyalty would remain strong because it always had. We learned—quickly—that nothing in a business stays strong without intentional leadership focus behind it.

Over time, the pursuit of profitability tightened, particularly after the company was acquired by two private equity firms. The emphasis on EBITDA grew, and the customer-loyalty dashboards that once inspired our coworkers to provide excellent service were replaced with the "EBITDA Meter." Which few understood. The global recession layered additional pressure on the system. Growth slowed. The strategy prioritized cost control and stability—common responses in both maturing companies and recessionary periods. Investments were reduced, hiring paused, and bonuses were constrained. The first layoffs in the company's history took place, and revenue targets became harder to reach.

None of this was the result of any one leader or one decision. It was the outcome of a complex combination of market forces, ownership expectations, organizational maturity, and the natural consequences of the priorities we collectively elevated.

The lesson?

Vision matters. Priorities shape behavior. And what you choose to aim for becomes what you inevitably build—sometimes in ways you don't see until the results arrive.

Vision: Where Emotion Meets Purpose

"Begin with the end in mind," said Stephen Covey, author of the famous self-help book *The 7 Habits of Highly Effective People*. Your vision is the picture of where you want to be. It is where everything comes together—where monumental success is imagined and deeply felt. It's the triumphant moment when you've climbed the mountain, braved the valley, tamed the dragon, and reached your ultimate destination.

The heroines and heroes are celebrated. The responsible parties are exalted as the most incredibly talented, expertly assembled team ever. The fruits of their labor are realized, and everyone benefits from the incredible vision being attained. In your vision, you and your team have reached the pinnacle.

But a truly brilliant vision is more than a finish line—it's a fire starter. It's not just about imagining success. It's about inspiring belief, igniting hearts, and giving people a reason to give their all. When vision resonates emotionally, it awakens something deeper than strategy ever could. It says, "This matters. You matter. We're doing something that will make a difference."

You may be asking yourself:

- "Is this vision good for others?"
- "Does it have a higher purpose?"
- "Is it inspiring?"
- "Is it motivating?"

People will move mountains for the noble cause, something they believe in. History and storytelling have proven it time and again. From epics to underdog comebacks, we're wired to rally behind a cause greater than ourselves. But here's the truth: until hearts are engaged, you won't get their best.

> "People don't buy what you do. They buy why you do it."
> —Simon Sinek

Ask yourself: "Is my vision noble?" A noble vision leads somewhere greater than personal gain. It's not about the almighty dollar. It's about serving others. Every. Single. Time.

> "What is the use of living, if it be not to strive for noble causes and to make this muddled world a better place for those who will live in it after we are gone?"
> —Winston Churchill

I'll be honest; this won't be easy. On the journey to brilliance, every leader will face moments of doubt, frustration, and fatigue. The pressure will mount. The headwinds will be strong. There will be days when you'll want to give up.

But this is where leaders are made. This is the crucible—where your purpose is tested and your character is forged. Vision is your guiding light through the dark tunnel. It's what reminds you, and your team, why the fight is worth it.

A game that ends 35–0 rarely inspires; it's the hard-fought 35–34 comeback win in double overtime that captures our hearts. That's what people remember. That's what motivates.

Brilliant vision is your invitation to write that kind of story. One that is bold. Emotional. Transformative. Don't just craft your vision with your head. Lead with your heart.

Let's Talk About Fear

It's completely normal—even expected—for a brilliant vision to scare the hell out of you. It should. In fact, if your vision doesn't make your heart race just a little, it's probably not bold enough.

At first glance, your vision might feel wildly impractical or too difficult to achieve. You may feel the urge to retreat to the "safe zone"—to set more reasonable, achievable goals that won't rock the boat. And that's understandable.

But pause and ask yourself:
- "Does that smaller, safer goal make my skin tingle with excitement?"
- "Does it make me slightly nervous in the best way?"
- "Does it light a fire inside me—or simply keep me warm?"

Chances are the safer goal feels comfortable—too comfortable. But comfort rarely leads to greatness.

The truth is that a safe goal doesn't stir hearts, spark innovation, or rally a team. It doesn't change the game. It doesn't transform you.

"The creative process is terrifying because you don't know what will happen or what new dangers or challenges you'll find. It takes security to have a spirit of adventure, discovery, and creativity."
—Stephen Covey

For me, the creative process is exhilarating. I love visioning. Dreaming big. Exploring what's possible. I often ask myself, "How far could this idea go? What's the biggest version of this?"

I know that's not everyone's default setting. Some leaders feel overwhelmed by vision work. That's why in BOLD leadership, we've designed a step-by-step process to help you clarify your vision without getting lost in the fear. It breaks it down so the big doesn't feel so impossible.

And still, let me be honest: I'm not immune to fear. I'm great at dreaming big, but I can also freeze when it's time to map out the details.

But my fear doesn't usually show up at the start; it shows up later, when the stakes get higher, when I start to ask, "Can I actually pull this off?"

Expert tips:
- **Remember the hard things you've done before.**
- **Call on your past grit. The courage. The growth. Remind yourself: you've done hard things before—you can do this too. Fear is part of the journey. But so is resilience.**
- **Take the first step. Then the next. With each step, the fear loses its grip and confidence takes its place.**

Brilliant vision isn't supposed to be easy—it's supposed to be worth it.

Clarifying Your Brilliant Vision: The Power of Knowing Your "One Big Thing"

One way to bring clarity to your Brilliant Vision is by using the Hedgehog Concept, made famous by Jim Collins in Good to Great. The idea comes from an ancient Greek parable: "The fox knows many things, but the hedgehog knows one big thing."

What does the hedgehog know? It knows that whenever the fox comes after it, there's no need to run in circles or try dozens of tricks. The hedgehog simply rolls into a ball, its spiny quills pointing outward, leaving the fox without any way to land the kill. The hedgehog wins not by doing everything, but by doing one thing—perfectly.

Leaders who operate like the hedgehog don't waste energy chasing every new idea or distraction. Instead, they lean into their core purpose, play to their greatest strength, and move with powerful simplicity and confidence. In a noisy, fast-moving world, that clarity of focus is what makes the hedgehog unstoppable.

Collins describes the Hedgehog Concept as the intersection of three key questions:

1. What are you deeply passionate about?
2. What can you be the best at in the world?
3. What drives your economic engine or fuels your impact?

When those three circles align, you've struck clarity gold. This is your "one big thing." Your brilliant vision becomes not only BOLD—but also deeply focused and incredibly powerful.

In BOLD leadership, we help leaders get to the core of that vision—not just what sounds good but what is truly worth building. The Hedgehog Concept gives you a framework to sift through the noise and say with confidence: "This is who we are. This is what we're here to do. This is where we're going."

You won't have all the answers. It's about anchoring your direction to something meaningful, differentiated, and sustainable.

BOLD vision becomes brilliant when it's clear. Clarity comes from focus. And focus begins when you know your one big thing.

Next, asking the right questions can guide your thinking and help ensure that the vision is both ambitious and achievable. Here are some important questions to consider:

- What is your ultimate goal?
  - What are you trying to achieve in the long term? This helps set the direction and purpose of the vision.
- Why is this vision important?
  - What value does this vision bring to your stakeholders, including customers, employees, and the community? Understanding the "why" inspires and motivates your team.
- What differentiates this vision from the competition?
  - How does your vision stand out in the market? What unique aspects or innovations do you bring to the table?
- Who are your main stakeholders, and how are they impacted?
  - Identifying and understanding the needs and expectations of different stakeholders ensures that the vision addresses relevant concerns and leverages potential partnerships.
- What are the potential challenges and obstacles?
  - What barriers might you face in achieving this vision, and how can you overcome them? Utilize as much information and data as you can gather: market, operational, financial, and technological landscapes and challenges.
- What resources will be required to achieve this vision?

- ○ Assessing needed resources such as capital, talent, and technology is crucial for realistic planning.
- How will you measure success?
  - ○ What metrics or milestones can you track as you progress toward the vision? This helps evaluate effectiveness and informs necessary adjustments. Leading and lagging indicators are both needed here. Leading indicators are the actions you will take to achieve the result, whereas lagging indicators measure what happened, or the actual result.
- What timeline is realistic for achieving this vision?
  - ○ Establishing a timeline helps set expectations and plan for step-by-step implementation.
- How does this vision align with your core values and culture?
  - ○ For seamless adoption and integration, the vision must be in harmony with the company's values and culture.
- What changes or innovations are required to realize this vision?
  - ○ Identifying the need for innovation in processes, products, and/or business models can help shape a transformative strategy.

These questions can form the foundation that clarifies and strengthens your vision, ensuring that it is bold and actionable.

Dare to Pursue Your Brilliant Vision

When you use a combination of the clarity tools—whether it's the Hedgehog Concept, your values, or purpose-driven storytelling—you are able to articulate your vision in a way that's inspiring, clear, and compelling.

The more you pursue your brilliant vision, the more confident you become. Each stretch outside your comfort zone builds capacity. Each step forward gives you the courage to take a bolder one next time.

Pursuing a brilliant vision beats chasing run-of-the-mill goals every time. Why? Because even if you fall short, the distance you travel will be far greater. You'll go further, grow faster, and create ripple effects that transform your organization and everyone in it.

This kind of focused effort doesn't just move the needle—it moves people. It builds momentum. And it shapes you into the kind of leader who doesn't settle for good enough.

Think about it: if the journey is this powerful, what's really holding you back from going all in?

Wolter Inc.'s Brilliant Vision: Transforming Today's Operational Expenses into Tomorrow's New Revenue Streams for Their Customers

Jerry Weidman is CEO of Wolter Inc., one of the largest and most diverse industrial-equipment and productivity-solutions providers in the country. Jerry and his team are on a BOLD mission to increase their diversification to provide a full solution to their material-handling clients. In one recent conversation, Jerry, a BOLD leader, outlined a strategic and transformative approach to leadership and business management, emphasizing the importance of foresight, adaptability, and strategic alignment with industry trends. His vision is rooted in understanding the trajectories of the industries he operates within and leveraging these insights to position his business for success over the next five years.

Jerry began by explaining the importance of envisioning the future state of the industry to guide business strategy: "I start with where I'm going to be in five years, what business is going to be . . . it's no different than a journey."

Jerry underscored the significance of aligning business strategies with industry trends such as consolidation, automation, and electrification, which have shaped his sector over the years. A critical part of his vision involves close collaboration with suppliers to align strategic intentions, ensuring that his business adapts to the evolving landscape. He went on to note, "My suppliers' perception of where they're going to take their business five years from now is important to me as well." This partnership is crucial for setting targets and measuring success across various metrics such as revenue and market share.

Jerry also discussed the evolution of his company's focus from product-based to solutions-oriented and finally to enhancing productivity.

This progression reflects his strategic shift toward more value-added offerings, encapsulated in his company's evolving taglines from "your sole source for material handling" to "accelerating your productivity."

Furthermore, he emphasizes the importance of assembling the right team and resources to execute the vision, drawing an analogy to the erstwhile TV show Mission Impossible. He's stated, "One of the first things they do after they're given the mission is the leader of the mission pulls out histories and bios of the people that it's going to take to accomplish."

Jerry's strategic thinking extends to acquisitions and organic growth, where he has pursued a consistent 10-percent growth rate, balancing various growth avenues with financial stability. His approach is methodical and well-informed, as he concluded, "I know by historic profitability I can keep my debt-to-equity ratio 3:1 or less. I can grow ad infinitum."

In summary, Jerry's BOLD vision is about setting lofty goals and meticulously planning and executing strategies that align with current resources and future industry directions. His approach highlights the necessity for strategic foresight, alignment with industry trends, and operational adaptability in crafting an ambitious and achievable vision. Jerry's BOLD leadership has not only enabled his company to grow quickly and successfully but also set it up for long-term growth and success.

Your Vision in Action

When your brilliant vision is clear, compelling, and connected to strategy, it becomes more than words on a wall. It becomes the heartbeat of your organization—the lens through which every decision is made.

Keep revisiting it. Refine as needed. And most importantly, use it to lead.

What's Next?

Your brilliant vision is bold, inspiring, and ready to guide you forward. But now comes the next chapter: execution. The journey from vision to reality is where real leadership happens.

In the following sections, we walk through the strategic road map to make your vision real—from setting aligned goals to tracking progress and celebrating wins. You'll get the tools to move from concept to action—and from action to impact.

Get ready. Your brilliant vision is just getting started.

BOLD Takeaways

- **Brilliant vision ignites transformation.** A bold, emotionally resonant vision doesn't just guide strategy—it fuels innovation, inspires action, and elevates performance. It moves people.

- **Play it safe: grow incrementally. Lead BOLDly: grow exponentially.** When leaders prioritize comfort, growth slows. When they pursue meaningful, daring visions, real momentum begins.

- **Clarity creates confidence.** Both tools such as the Hedgehog Concept and BOLD reflection help you articulate a vision that is clear, compelling, and focused on your "one big thing."

- **Fear is a signal that you're on the right path.** A brilliant vision should stretch you. If it doesn't feel a little scary, it's probably not BOLD enough. Step forward anyway—the payoff is worth it.

Chapter 1:
Create Your Brilliant Vision Exercise

Reflect on these prompts to deepen your understanding of bold vision and help shape your own. Then, draft your own.

Reflection Prompts

1. What's my "one big thing"?
If I could only accomplish one brilliant goal in the next three to five years, what would it be—and why does it matter?

2. When have I been most inspired by a vision—either my own or someone else's?
What made it powerful or memorable?

3. What is my personal or team's version of "landing among the stars"?
What would success look like if I aimed higher than I'd ever dared before?

4. What beliefs or fears are holding me back from dreaming bigger?
Where am I playing it safe—and what would it take to step into BOLDness?

5. How clear is my current vision?
Could I explain it in one sentence that inspires others to rally behind it?

6. What would make my vision not just good but *brilliant*?
Think of the qualities discussed: inspiring, meaningful, valuable, impactful, above the norm, rooted in deep care.

7. Who else needs to see and believe in my vision?
How can I invite them to shape, support, and amplify it?

Take your time with these. A brilliant vision is worth the reflection.

Crafting Your Brilliant Vision Statement: Action Steps

A brilliant vision isn't just inspirational—it's strategic. It becomes a decision filter, a unifier, and a force multiplier. When clearly articulated, it simplifies complexity, attracts support, and rallies people toward a shared future. Here's how to shape yours:

1. Clarify Your Ultimate Goal

Start by asking yourself:

"What do we want to be known for?"

"What long-term impact do we want to make?"

This is your North Star. It gives your vision direction and anchors it in purpose.

2. Reflect and Research

Look inward and outward. Use the questions from earlier in this chapter to reflect on your values, passions, and aspirations. Pair that with insight from market trends, customer needs, and future possibilities. This balance of soul-searching and strategy ensures that your vision is both inspired and informed.

3. Blend Experience with Innovation

Pull lessons from past wins and setbacks. Then challenge yourself: what new possibilities could emerge if we dared to think bigger? A brilliant vision honors where you've been, but it's driven by where you're going.

4. Draft Your Vision Statement

Now put it into words. Your vision should be the following:

- Bold—aim high
- Clear—free of jargon
- Present tense—as if it's already happening
- Meaningful—connected to your purpose

Test it: Does it inspire? Does it stretch you? Would others rally around it?

5. Involve Others

Invite trusted voices in. Collaboration strengthens clarity. Gather feedback from your team, advisors, and stakeholders. Their insights can help you refine your message—and build early ownership.

6. Finalize and Communicate

Polish the statement based on feedback. Then share it. Widely. Repeatedly. Visibly. Leaders breathe life into vision by making it part of daily conversation, decision-making, and storytelling.

7. Align Goals and Strategy

Your vision is the *why*. Now build the *how*. Set priorities, define success metrics, and create initiatives that are aligned with your vision. Ensure that every team, project, and resource is driving toward the same destination.

Engaging Others in the Brilliant Vision

"If you want to go fast, go alone.
If you want to go far, go together."
—African proverb

One of the most powerful ways to move a vision forward is to connect others to it. BOLD leaders find ways to engage everyone in the vision. To take it a step further, including your employees/team members in the creation process automatically creates buy-in. Many heads are generally better than one when formulating a brilliant vision.

To inspire others to act on the brilliant vision, they need to feel like it is worthy of their focus and attention and make a personal connection to it. When they understand the why and what's in it for them, you can capture their hearts and minds; when hearts are engaged in a brilliant vision, people will do whatever it takes and bust through walls to achieve it.

A Transformational Journey

One of our clients, a rising leader in the business side of college athletics, transitioned from top individual contributor to team leader. Though she excelled personally, her team initially achieved only 85 percent of their revenue goal, and morale was low—some even questioned her leadership. She felt frustrated, knowing that her own potential wasn't yet reflected in the team's results.

Through a yearlong executive-coaching engagement, we conducted a 360 review and gathered performance data. Together, we crafted a brilliant vision: to become one of the top-performing teams in the nation and win the company's prestigious team award. This clear, compelling goal became a rallying point for both the leader and her team.

Over the course of the engagement, she grew into her leadership, driving accountability, modeling the vision, and inspiring her team. Performance steadily improved, and the results spoke for themselves:

Key Performance Indicator	Start	Conclusion	Change
Revenue Goal	85%	115%	+30
Leader Rating	3	4.3	+1.3
Employee Engagement	50	75	+25

The transformation was profound. By anchoring her leadership in a BOLD, aspirational vision, she elevated her effectiveness, aligned her team, and reignited engagement. What began as frustration turned into momentum—and positioned her team as strong contenders for the top national award.

Lesson: a clear, motivating vision not only improves performance metrics but also transforms team culture, confidence, and collective belief in what's possible.

Don'ts and Don'ts

Brilliant visions move forward when others are energized and mobilized by the promise of what is to come. When everyone is engaged, they will work diligently to do their part in making the team's goals come to fruition. And I use the word "engage" intentionally to establish a meaningful contact or connection with something.

When team members feel connected to something bigger than themselves, they are committed and will work long and hard to bring the vision to life. This is the difference between a committed team versus a merely compliant one. In the days when command and control were the favorite tactics of leaders (yes, I know there are still many such leaders out there today), compliance was the goal.

"I say, 'Jump'—you say, 'How high?' That's how this works."
—Ben Affleck's character in *Boiler Room*

Management by fear of consequences and repercussions all too often used to be the norm. *If you don't do what I say, there will be punishment.* Employees would practice avoidance when they knew someone was watching. Instead, there should be a common goal to gain commitment, which means being dedicated to a vision, putting people on a better path to engagement and, ultimately, achievement.

I once worked for a company that had an employee manual titled *Dos and Don'ts*. Tongue in cheek, we referred to it humorously as *Don'ts and Don'ts* because that is really what it was: a list of everything we should **not** do. It did very little for employee morale, let alone get buy-in on the vision. All it contained were directives and consequences. This reminds me of leaders who have taken the time and trouble to create a brilliant vision but failed to enlist others. Employees get told what to do or not to do *a lot*. Even in life, rules are created that must be followed everywhere: when we drive, shop, bank, engage with fellow humans, walk our dogs, and, especially, are at work. Though some may thrive in highly regulated settings, many do not. Yet brilliant visions are best mobilized through inspiration, not command, regulation, and fear of consequences.

In 2016, I had the privilege of meeting the remarkable Judith E. Glaser at a coaching conference where she held an enlightening session on the profound connection between building trust, high performance, and workplace communication. Her presentation was so compelling that I eagerly joined the long queue at her book signing to get a copy of her work, *Conversational Intelligence*. Not only did

Judith graciously sign my book, but we also had a meaningful discussion about how her research complemented that of Daniel Goleman and other scholars in emotional intelligence.

As I delved into her book, one concept particularly resonated with me: instructing someone can trigger an increase in stress hormones such as cortisol, epinephrine, and norepinephrine. Conversely, engaging someone with questions and fostering a positive dialogue can boost pleasure hormones such as dopamine, oxytocin, and endorphins. This revelation was a turning point for me.

It is especially relevant when considering engaging others in a brilliant vision. It highlights the psychological and physiological benefits of inviting team members to participate in a constructive conversation rather than simply dictating actions. Engaging others through inquiry supports a harmonious work environment and aligns with our natural biological responses, enhancing collaboration and a shared commitment to the vision. Whew—that's powerful!

The Importance of Communicating a Clear Vision and Miller's Law: The Power of Seven

A common mistake leaders make is to communicate their vision once and expect everyone to remember it. One leader shared with me in a moment of frustration, "I told everyone in the town-hall meeting at the beginning of the year. Why aren't they getting it?!"

Some leaders get upset when they find that their teams and organization don't remember their vision or get it wrong. But here's the problem: communication is rarely one and done. Especially when you want to enlist others in your brilliant vision, you must share it often and in such an inspiring manner that they hear it, understand it, and buy in. A concept known as Miller's Law is applied in the marketing world as a fundamental that states that the buyer should see or hear your marketing message at least seven times before they buy it from you.[i] Ensuring this number of exposures can help solidify your vision for your team and ensure consistency and clarity.

You must also understand that people learn through different modes: visual, auditory, experiential, reading, writing, and others. The more methods you use, the more likely your vision will be understood by all. Engage your early adopters and influencers to build enthusiasm and commitment to the vision. Use your employees with large followings within the company to create coalitions of supporters; they can effectively get the message out and encourage buy-in. Most importantly, put your vision communication on repeat. They need to hear it often to underscore the importance and ensure clarity. Develop a communications plan to ensure that they are truly absorbing it.

When you share a clear, straightforward vision that grabs people, you also answer your team's big questions: "What does success look like? What's in it for me?"

Take Ernest Shackleton, for example. Legend has it that in the early 1900s, he posted an ad for his risky Antarctic trip that went something like this: "Men wanted. For hazardous journey, small wages, bitter cold, long months of complete darkness, constant danger, safe return doubtful, honor and recognition in case of success."

Even though the ad didn't sugarcoat the dangers, loads of people signed up. Perhaps the promise of "honor and recognition in case of success" struck a chord. It shows that we're drawn to be part of something bigger than ourselves, especially when there's a chance to make a real impact and get some recognition for it. And speaking of Shackleton, his vision not only guided them through seemingly insurmountable obstacles but also brought every single crew member back home safely against all odds. When they could see the opportunity to be part of something bigger, they joined eagerly.

That's where a communication plan comes in. It's not just about what you say—it's about how, when, and through whom you say it. A communication plan ensures that your message is consistent, intentional, and reinforced over time. At a high level, it outlines your key messages, identifies your audiences (both internal and external), selects the best channels to reach them (emails, team meetings, town halls, videos, Slack, etc.), and builds a cadence of communication. It should also highlight your champions—those influential voices in your organization who can amplify the vision—and include space for two-way feedback to keep the message alive and adaptive. Think of it as your map for cascading the vision, aligning your messengers, and making sure your team doesn't just hear the message once—they live it.

Connect the Team Personally to the Vision: Belay System

A belay device is what keeps climbers secure as they ascend and descend a rock face. It's made up of ropes, harnesses, and carabiners that adjust with a climber's movement—providing just enough freedom to explore, with the safety needed to take bold steps. In leadership, your brilliant vision is the belay. It anchors your team while giving them the confidence to climb.

Expert tip: provide your team with the compelling reason they need to trust and follow you.

A well-crafted vision—one that's clear, inspiring, and personal—becomes that reason. When people see themselves in the vision and understand how their everyday efforts help make it a reality, that's when commitment ignites. That's when they climb with you.

To unlock their highest performance, passion, and effort, your people need more than clarity—they need personal engagement. They need to see how their strengths, goals, and values align with the bigger picture. When they feel deeply connected to the vision—when it matters to them—they don't just participate; they commit. That's the moment when good teams become great and bold outcomes become possible.

How can you connect your team to your brilliant vision? By asking brilliant questions, of course:

1. What part of our vision resonates most with you—and why?
   (What excites or inspires you about where we're headed?)
2. Think about a time when you were deeply motivated to achieve a goal. What made that experience meaningful for you?
   (What can we learn from that to connect your work to our vision?)
3. What does personal success look like for you—and how might it align with the goals of our team or organization?

(Let's explore where your aspirations and our vision intersect.)

4. Where do you see strong alignment between your strengths or goals and our vision—and where might there be gaps?
(This helps us ensure that your contributions are both impactful and fulfilling.)

5. How can I support you in bringing our vision to life?
(What do you need from me to stay engaged, empowered, and energized?)

When you clearly understand each team member, you can hook them into the vision using the belay—keeping them securely connected while giving them both the freedom to contribute through their strengths and the confidence to reach higher.

Keep Your Brilliant Vision Front and Center

Using dashboards and visual aids is like having a GPS for your brilliant vision—they keep what you want within your line of sight and help everyone stay on track.

1. **Picture your success.** Kick things off by visually mapping where you want to go. A vision board works great for this, showing your end goals in a way that's easy to get excited about every day. Alongside this, set up some key performance indicators (KPIs) that track your progress, both now and down the road.

2. **Pick the right KPIs.** Think about the KPIs that will push the needle on your goals. You'll need numbers and percentages (quantitative KPIs), but don't overlook the value of feedback (qualitative KPIs)—both are key to seeing how well you're doing. Example: Say your vision is to make your team the top-performing in the company. What needs to happen? You might need to enhance team collaboration, increase client satisfaction, or improve project delivery times. For each of these areas, set specific KPIs to gauge effectiveness. Track these metrics closely to see what's boosting your team's performance and where you might need to pivot.

3. **Keep tabs and tweak as needed.** Think of your KPIs like a rear-view mirror—they're lag indicators, showing what's already happened. They help you see the results of past actions: revenue earned, projects completed, and customers retained. But if you're hitting your targets and still not getting closer to the big picture, it's time to adjust.

That's where lead indicators come in. They're the forward-looking signals that predict future success. They are the behaviors and activities you can influence right now—like the number of prospect meetings, employee check-ins, or innovation sprints. When you track both lead and lag indicators together, you don't just measure outcomes—you steer performance in real time.

Lead vs Lag Indicators

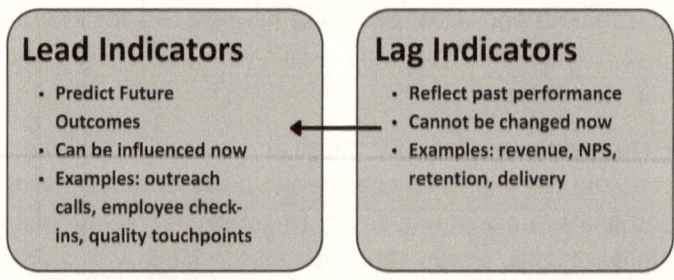

Lead Indicators
- Predict Future Outcomes
- Can be influenced now
- Examples: outreach calls, employee check-ins, quality touchpoints

Lag Indicators
- Reflect past performance
- Cannot be changed now
- Examples: revenue, NPS, retention, delivery

By weaving these tools into your planning, you can keep a sharp eye on your goals, measure your steps, and shift your strategies without missing a beat. That way, every move you make is a step closer to where you want to be.

The BOLD vision of Rosemary Swierk, CEO of Direct Steel and Construction, began serendipitously when she decided to purchase and rehabilitate a dilapidated building she would regularly pass during her commute. This initial venture into real estate development marked the start of her company's expansion into creating and improving properties, which evolved into forming two separate development companies. Her vision continued to evolve as opportunities arose, leading her to become a general contractor for others, further diversifying her business during the economic downturn of 2007–2008. During this period, she strategically focused on Direct Steel to leverage market opportunities, notably seizing on the American Recovery Act to pivot into government contracts.

A defining moment for her and her company was the decision to pursue government work, despite initial challenges in gaining experience. Holding onto this vision led Rosemary to secure significant contracts with the Department of Defense and other public and private entities, enhancing her company's reputation and capabilities. Throughout her career, she has demonstrated a clear vision for spotting opportunities and a robust process for pursuing them, even in uncertain times. Her leadership style is characterized by a balance between a strong visionary drive and a collaborative approach, emphasizing the importance of aligning her team with the company's vision and effectively communicating this vision to ensure that everyone understands and shares it. This approach has allowed her to successfully navigate her company through various market cycles and challenges, consistently aligning her actions with her strategic vision for growth and resilience.

BOLD Takeaways

- **Brilliant visions thrive when others feel personally connected to them.** When people are involved in shaping the vision, they're more likely to own it, fight for it, and rally others around it.

- **Leaders who lead with vision and inquiry inspire higher performance than those who rely on command and control do.** As Judith E. Glaser taught us, ask, don't just tell. Engagement drives dopamine; directives drive cortisol.

- **Communicating your vision once is not enough.** Use Miller's Law: people need to hear a message at least seven times in order to internalize it. Use multiple modalities and messengers to reinforce the vision until it sticks.

- **Tracking lead and lag indicators ensures that your brilliant vision stays front and center—and that your progress is real.** Vision boards inspire, KPIs measure, and dashboards keep the whole team aligned and climbing together.

Keep Your Brilliant Vision Front and Center

Using dashboards and visual aids is like having a GPS for your brilliant vision—they keep what you want right in your line of s sight and help everyone stay on track. More on this later.

1 Picture Your Success

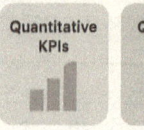
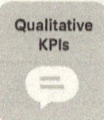

Kick things off by visually mapping where you want to go. A vision board works great for this, showing your end goals in a way that's easy to get excited about every day. Alongside this, set up some Key Performance Indicators (KPIs) that track your progress, both now and down the road.

2 Pick the Right KPIs

Quantitative KPIs

Qualitative KPIs

Think about the KPIs that will push the needle on your goals. You'll need numbers and percentages (quantitative KPIs) but don't overlook the value of feedback (qualitative KPIs)—both are key to seeing how well you're doing.

3 Keep Tabs and Tweak as Needed

Think of your KPIs like a rearview mirror—they're lag indicators, showing what's already happemed. But if you're hitting your targets and still not getting closer to the big picture, it's time to adjust.

Brilliant vision dashboard

Chapter 2:
Engaging Others in the
Brilliant Vision Exercise

Instructions

Section 1: Vision Statement Overview. Briefly describe the essence of the brilliant vision. This should be a clear and inspiring statement that captures the future direction of the company and/or your team.

Section 2: Why This Vision? Purpose and Importance. Explain why this vision was developed and what its importance is to the future of the company. Outline the key benefits of embracing this vision for the company and its employees.

Section 3: Key Objectives/Major Goals. List the major goals that the brilliant vision aims to achieve. Use bullet points for clarity. Provide a timeline or road map of key milestones in achieving the vision.

Section 4: Role of Team Members' Individual Contributions. Describe how each team member can contribute to achieving the vision. Clearly state what is expected from them during the implementation of the vision.

Section 5: Methods of Communication Channels. Specify the channels through which the vision will be communicated and discussed (e.g., meetings, emails, internal newsletters). Encourage feedback and describe how team members can provide their input or ask questions.

Section 6: Provide Resources. List resources available to help team members understand and implement the vision (e.g., training sessions, documents, direct support from leaders). Detail any support structures in place, such as mentorship programs or special committees, to aid in the adoption of the vision.

Section 7: Monitoring and Updates/Progress Tracking. Explain how progress toward the vision will be monitored and measured. Commit to regular updates on the vision's implementation progress. Motivate the team with a final call to action that reinforces their role in making the vision a reality.

Brilliant Vision	• Add your Brilliant Vision Statement here
Why	• Why this vision?
When	• Start Date: • End Date:
Key Objectives	• List the major goals that the "Brilliant Vision" aims to achieve.
Team Member Roles	• Who does what • Expectations
Methods of Communication	• Channels, feedback, interactions
Resources Needed	• What resources and/or support structures will be needed?
Progress Tracking	• Measure progress, provide updates, call to action

Brilliant vision outline

Chapter 3

The Journey to Achieve Your Brilliant Vision

In the CEO's office, a glowing neon sign delivered
a powerful message:
"Begin. The rest is easy."

Starting the journey toward a brilliant vision can feel overwhelming. In the early 2000s, John Edwardson was CEO of CDW, a leading provider of technology services and solutions, and had a sign on his credenza to remind himself—and others—that you don't need 100-percent clarity or all of the answers in order to begin. His rule of thumb? If you have 80 percent of the information, GO! Waiting for the final 20 percent often leads to delays, overthinking, and decisions that don't change with more data.

The real challenge is bridging the gap between where you are today and where your vision will lead. Taking that first bold step without a perfectly mapped-out plan can feel scary and counterintuitive. But experienced leaders know that clarity often comes through action, not before it. Taking a cautious, overly risk-averse approach often leads to analysis paralysis—the dream dies before it ever begins. Build your plan, start the journey, and be willing to adjust as you go.

Once your plan is in motion, the next challenge is letting go. Many leaders fall into the trap of micromanaging, hovering over every detail to ensure "perfection." In CDW's early days, its founder, Michael P. Krasny, was quoted as saying,

> "Perfection is unattainable. If you strive for perfection,
> you'll achieve excellence."

That still holds true today. Here's the reality: the more you try to micromanage, the more you limit your team and hold back progress. You become the bottleneck.

Command-and-control leadership may drive compliance and short-term wins, but it won't unlock bold growth and pursuit of your brilliant vision—and it will almost certainly lead to burnout and attrition.

Empower your team. Trust them. That's how you build lasting momentum and unleash excellence.

Exponential growth comes from vision.

Incremental growth comes from control.

Exponential growth starts with a brilliant vision—and the courage to execute it. Clarity doesn't come from waiting; it comes from moving. As you put the plan into action, things come into focus: the goals become clearer, responsibilities get sharper, and your team feels empowered to use their strengths to drive results.

Empowerment is the game-changer. Let your team own the how while you lead the what. This mindset shift—from control to trust—is one of the biggest (and most rewarding) transitions a leader can make.

The secret? Give your team a strong plan and the freedom to execute. Stay close enough to support and coach, but not so close that you stifle creativity or ownership.

And remember: mistakes and missteps will happen. They are not failures—they are feedback. They make sure that the learnings stick and that your team grows stronger, bolder, and better.

You Can Beg for Forgiveness

My leadership career began when I was tapped to become a sales manager. Along with the promotion, I was also tasked with launching an exciting new division. The company was looking to expand offerings and sell Apple and related products. Starting this new market turned into the beginning of an 18-year stint launching new division after new division at the fast-growing tech company where I worked. Each time, I felt a surge of excitement, quickly followed by an overwhelming sense of fear. There was literally no road map. I mostly loved—but also occasionally loathed—the freedom that came with so little guidance. The autonomy was exhilarating, but without oversight, I would agonize about which direction to take and, of course, at times I led my team down the wrong path. My first task of building a new market was also my first experience in management. I reported directly to the company president, and I had a million questions. I made multiple trips to his office, list in hand, asking, "What about this? What about that?" He indulged me the first couple of times, but during my third visit, he slid my list aside, looked me straight in the eyes, and said something I'll never forget: "Kim, if I have to make all the decisions, one of us isn't needed."

I was stunned. I was 25 years old with **zero** experience in leading and building new markets. But he believed in me and wanted me to lead—not just execute. I nervously asked, "What if I mess up?" He smiled and said, "Then you can beg for forgiveness."

What he knew—long before I did—was that the risks were small and the reward was big growth. His confidence in me gave me the clarity and courage to move forward, make decisions, and build something from the ground up. It was the kind of vote of confidence that changes the course of a career. I did end up begging for forgiveness many times. And in the end, those were some of the lessons I learned best.

Leadership vs. Management

Let's make an important distinction: leadership and management are not the same—and understanding the difference between the two can free you from holding yourself back.

Leadership is primarily a right-brain activity: creative, visionary, and inspiring. It's about imagining the future, thinking big, and daring to dream "one size too big" for yourself and your team. It's fueled by possibility and purpose.

Management, on the other hand, is a left-brain activity focused on processes, systems, and execution. It's about structure, efficiency, and getting things done.

Too often, leaders feel that they need to handle all the management tasks before they "earn" the right to be visionary. It's comforting to check boxes and clear the deck—that's the achiever in us.

But here's the truth: though management is important, it's not your most important work as a leader. Vision must come first. Only then can you align people, systems, and action toward something truly bold.

Can you lead and manage at the same time?

Sure—but it's far more effective to divide and conquer. And not just within your own mind. Bring in many minds. Leadership is not a solo act.

Here's the key distinction:

Leaders own the *what*. They cast the vision.

Managers own the *how*. They build the plan and make it happen.

Management (Execution)	Leadership (Vision)
Owns the *how*	Owns the *what*
Details the plan	Dreams big
Drives results	Inspires action
Ensures consistency	Encourages creativity

Trying to lead through management—starting with the details— can trap you in the weeds. You'll lose the energy, the momentum, and the big-picture clarity that's essential for bold growth.

Visionary leaders who embrace creativity and calculated risk are the ones who stretch further and grow faster. They're not waiting for the full road map—they're confident that they can figure it out along the way. Such confidence creates empowerment.

In contrast, a management-heavy mindset that clings to rigid plans and predictable steps often stalls progress—especially in today's ever-shifting environment.

The truth is that no leader has it all figured out. That's part of the adventure. But when you unite a team around a shared vision and trust them to navigate the path together, you can handle anything that comes your way.

Build Your Plan: Road Map

This is what it's like to go after your brilliant vision: exhilarating and scary. You are on the road less traveled, so the road map essentially doesn't exist. In order to get from where you are to where you want to go, it is up to you and possibly the team to figure it out. Over time, I've formulated a standard road map that has helped me build each plan:

1. Research and SWOT
2. Hypotheses / Plans A, B, and C
3. RACI, KPIs, Progress Tracking

Research and SWOT

You don't know what you don't know, so get curious, get out there, and learn as quickly as possible. Go to trusted data sources such as peer-reviewed journals, read books, and access research collected by government agencies, think tanks, and professional organizations. Some favorites of mine are Gartner Research, McKinsey & Company, Deloitte Insights, Forrester Research, and *Harvard Business Review*.

Next, spend time talking to the people within the industry/function. The information I've collected has fed into the strategy I've developed on what products to sell, where to buy them, what to buy with them in order to create solutions, our go-to-market strategy, what media we should use to reach our audience, whom to hire, how to set up onboarding/training, and a lot more.

Now create a SWOT (strengths, weaknesses, opportunities, and threats) analysis from what you have learned. What are the strengths and weaknesses of your brilliant vision? Where are the threats? Where are the best growth opportunities?

Expert tip: utilizing your hedgehog, which we talked about in chapter 1, is a great way to maximize the opportunity in front of you.

Hypotheses

Don't just build one plan—build three: Plan A, Plan B, and maybe even a bold Plan C. Then ask:

- "What are the strengths and risks of each?"
- "Where can we gain scale?"
- "How much effort and investment does each require?"

Without sounding like Captain Obvious, of course you should do this: start with the plan that gets you closest to your brilliant vision with the least friction—lowest effort, highest return.

Then pressure-test it. Share your ideas with trusted advisors and cross-functional stakeholders. Include both champions who can refine it and critics who might poke holes. You need both perspectives to sharpen your thinking and strengthen the plan.

RACI and KPIs

Before you flip past this section because you fear that I will bore you to death with accountability abbreviations, know that I am not a person who lives in spreadsheets and project plans. Truth be told, I'm a big-picture, brilliant-vision whiteboard person every time, but I also know that we need measurement or else the vision may never leave the wall. Measurement and accountability are critical to ensure that the plan to achieve the vision stays on track.

RACI stands for "responsible, accountable, consulted, and informed" and is a great way to keep track of who owns and weighs in on what. That way, everyone knows who has the ball and who gets to put in their two cents.

KPIs are very important to ensure that progress is being made. Some obvious KPIs are revenue growth, profitability improvement, and new customer acquisition. Less-obvious ones might be product-line extension, client penetration, etc. As stated earlier, the more obvious and visible KPIs are, the better. If everyone understands exactly what they need to do to make the KPIs move in the right direction, then you are on the right track.

Work the Plan—but Stay in the Right Forest

Stephen Covey tells the story of a team of loggers working hard under the guidance of their managers. Productivity is high, trees are falling, and everything looks efficient. Then a voice calls out from above—someone standing on a mountain overlooking the forest:

The Leader: "Hey! You down there!"

The Team: "We're busy and making great progress!"

The Leader: "**Wrong forest!**"

This is the perfect illustration, back to the difference between **leadership** and **management**.

Management focuses on doing things right. Leadership ensures that the **right things** are being done.

As a leader, your job is to stay up on the mountain—holding the vision, seeing the bigger picture. Empower your team to execute the plan. Let them chop. Let them problem-solve. Your role is to check in with perspective, recognize effort, celebrate smart moves, and guide only when it matters most.

Don't get lost in the trees. Your team needs you to lead from the mountaintop.

Embolden the Plan

Back in my early days in corporate, I had a paperweight on my desk that read, *What would you do if you knew you could not fail?* It was an excellent reminder to reach further, strive more, and take the calculated risks necessary to achieve a brilliant vision.

Up your adventure level by emboldening your plan. Make it go further and faster and create more impact. Ask yourself these questions to make that happen:

- What would the plan look like if it were more courageous?
- How can we increase or decrease the speed of impact?
- What can I do instead of or in addition to what I've already planned?
- What will we need to happen in order for the plan's execution to be expedited?

- What resources will be needed?
- What are the risks?
- How do I mitigate risks?

No Plan (Perfectly) Survives Contact with Reality

Even the best plans will go sideways—sometimes subtly, sometimes dramatically. Timing shifts. Market conditions change. Assumptions are proven to be off. It's not a matter of *if* but *when*.

Think of it like driving. Even when you are headed down a seemingly straight road, you still have to constantly steer, making small corrections in order to stay in your lane. The same is true for leadership plans. This is the essence of contingency planning.

Sometimes the adjustments are minor—a tweak here or there. Other times, you need a full reset. And yes, occasionally, you'll have to scrap your plan entirely and start fresh. It may feel like failure, but it's just part of staying responsive and resilient.

Let's Tie It Back To KPI's

- **3% off? Probably a micro-adjustment will do**

- **30% off? That's a bigger signal. It is time for a major pivot - or a shift to Plan B**

The key is to build adaptive discipline—knowing when to stay the course, when to steer only slightly, and when to change lanes entirely.

Overcoming Obstacles: Plan B

Every plan—no matter how well thought out—will encounter obstacles. Some are external, but many are internal. One of the biggest? Head FUD—the fear, uncertainty, and doubt we generate in our own minds. These are often the most paralyzing yet also the most conquerable with a clear, actionable plan.

Then come the people challenges. Collaboration can be tough. When partnerships strain or stall, don't ignore it—instead, lean in. Spend time understanding others' goals, needs, and perspectives. Strong relationships are often the bridge that gets a plan back on track.

That said, here's the truth: You don't need a perfect plan or endless hours. You need consistent action. One hour a day—first thing, before the chaos sets in—can move mountains. What if you gave your vision that one bold hour?

Don't shut down possibilities just because the path feels unclear. If the current path is cluttered or blocked, maybe there's a better one waiting to be discovered. Visionary leaders don't wait for the fog to lift—they take action that clears it.

> *"Don't wish it were easier; wish you were better."*
> —Darren Hardy, *The Compound Effect*

Common Obstacles to Achieving a Brilliant Vision (and How to Overcome Them)

1. FUD (Fear, Uncertainty, Doubt)
Obstacle: Internal narratives such as "What if I fail?" or "I'm not ready."
How to overcome:
- Break goals into small, manageable steps.
- Reframe fear as helpful feedback: what is it pointing you toward?
- Build confidence through consistent action, not perfection.

2. People Problems

Obstacle: Misalignment, difficult dynamics, or friction when collaborating

How to overcome:

- Approach others with curiosity—learn their goals and drivers.
- Identify shared priorities and build alignment.
- Invest in relationships before rushing to outcomes.

3. Lack of Focus

Obstacle: Competing priorities or distractions diluting energy

How to overcome:

- Recenter on the plan—make it visible and front of mind.
- Use a daily "What's my one bold move?" reflection.
- Eliminate low-value tasks and distractions.

4. Mistaking Mistakes for Failure

Obstacle: Viewing setbacks as reasons to stop rather than to adapt

How to overcome:

- Treat mistakes as learning moments.
- Ask, "What worked? What didn't? What's next?"
- Reconnect to your purpose and long-term goal.

5. Lost Momentum

Obstacle: Inconsistent progress or lack of daily traction

How to overcome:

- Dedicate one hour each morning to focused action on your vision.
- Acknowledge and celebrate wins—even the small ones.
- Create systems that support sustained effort.

6. Resource Gaps

Obstacle: Not enough time, tools, funding, or support

How to overcome:

- Focus on high-impact actions that require minimal resources.
- Simplify: what's the most essential version of the plan?
- Engage allies who can help fill the gaps.

7. Low Grit

Obstacle: Giving up too soon or losing motivation

How to overcome:

- Reconnect with the why behind your vision regularly.
- Track and share progress in order to stay accountable.
- Surround yourself with people who support and challenge you.

There Are Lessons in Those Deep Scars

Have you ever heard the phrase "fail fast"? It's a powerful way of operating—because staying too long on a path that isn't working doesn't just waste time and resources; it also drains momentum and morale. And yet sunk costs can be a trap. Many leaders continue down the wrong path solely to justify past investments, even when they know it's time to pivot.

That's why it's essential to have clear criteria to assess progress and recognize when it's time to change direction. When something's off track, act quickly. Course-correct with intention.

When failure happens—and it will—don't sweep it aside. Pause for an after-action review. Ask, "What did I learn? What would I do differently next time?" Such a reflection turns setbacks into stepping stones.

Eleanor Roosevelt said it best: "You gain strength, courage, and confidence by every experience in which you really stop to look fear in the face. You are able to say to yourself, 'I lived through this horror. I can take the next thing that comes along.' You must do the thing you think you cannot do."

Failure may leave scars, but it also builds the strength to face what's next. I've found that the more I've learned from what didn't work, the more confident I've become in my ability to navigate what's ahead.

When the going gets tough, remember: You've been in hot water before. You came through it. And you came through stronger.

BOLD Takeaways

- **Start before you're ready.** Clarity comes through action. Don't wait for the perfect plan; begin with 80 percent and adjust as you go. Momentum builds confidence.

- **Lead the *what* and empower the *how*.** Visionary leaders set direction, not instructions. Empower your team with trust, not control. That's how you unlock exponential growth.

- **Make plans; then make them bolder.** A solid plan gets you started. A bold plan accelerates impact. Ask, "What would this look like if it were a bigger stretch?"

- **Failure isn't the end; it's the edge of growth.** Expect missteps. Learn fast. Adjust boldly. The lessons you learn through setbacks will shape you into being a strong leader.

Chapter 3:
SWOT Analysis Exercise for BOLD Leaders

Objective: To identify and leverage internal strengths and opportunities, while acknowledging and mitigating potential weaknesses and threats, in order to effectively strategize and realize a brilliant vision

Materials Needed:
- Whiteboard or large paper
- Markers or pens
- Sticky notes
- SWOT analysis template (divided into four quadrants: strengths, weaknesses, opportunities, threats)

Time Required: 1 to 2 hours
Participants: Leadership and/or team members

Instructions

1. Set the Context (5 minutes):
Briefly explain the purpose and goals of the SWOT analysis.
Reiterate the brilliant vision to ensure alignment throughout the exercise.

2. Identify Strengths (15 minutes):
Question: What internal resources and capabilities do we currently possess that can help us achieve our vision?
Action: Write each strength on a sticky note and place it in the strengths quadrant. Consider areas such as unique skills, intellectual property, strong network, team capabilities, financial resources, etc.

3. Identify Weaknesses (15 minutes):
Question: What are the limitations or gaps in our organization that could hinder us from achieving our vision?
Action: Write each weakness on a sticky note and place it in the weaknesses quadrant. Think about resource limitations, skills gaps, financial constraints, etc.

4. Identify Opportunities (15 minutes):

Question: What external opportunities exist that we can exploit in order to achieve our vision?

Action: Write each opportunity on a sticky note and place it in the opportunities quadrant. Consider market trends, economic shifts, technological advances, partnerships, etc.

5. Identify Threats (15 minutes):

Question: What external challenges could jeopardize our ability to achieve our vision?

Action: Write each threat on a sticky note and place it in the threats quadrant. Look at competitive pressures, market volatility, regulatory changes, etc.

6. Prioritize and Plan (30 minutes):

Review all items in each quadrant.

Prioritize the top three items in each category that have the highest impact on achieving the vision.

Question: How can we use our strengths to seize the identified opportunities and counteract the threats? How can we minimize or eliminate our weaknesses?

Action: Develop action items for the top priorities. Assign team members to take responsibility for each action.

7. Develop a Strategy (30 minutes):

Using the insights from the SWOT analysis, outline a strategic plan that addresses how to leverage strengths, improve weaknesses, capitalize on opportunities, and mitigate threats.

Ensure that the strategy is aligned with achieving the brilliant vision.

8. Review and Provide Feedback (10 minutes):

Present the strategy to the group for feedback.

Make adjustments based on the discussion in order to finalize the strategic plan.

Outcome: Participants will leave the exercise with a clear strategic plan that not only aligns with the brilliant vision but also is informed by a comprehensive understanding of the organization's internal dynamics and external environment.

Follow-Up: Schedule regular review sessions to assess progress against the strategy, adjust as necessary, and ensure that the organization remains aligned with the vision.

Oneness

Building a Foundation of Self-Awareness

"Be yourself; everyone else is taken."
—Oscar Wilde

Leading with self-awareness, authenticity, and integrity is the power of oneness. It empowers YOU to do YOU! It is the "O" in BOLD leadership. Your leadership power is derived from this trifecta of knowing who you are, being true to yourself, and aligning your actions accordingly.

The foundation of oneness is being the best version of you. Your way of being is unique and the biggest source of your strength. The more you try to be someone you are not, the weaker you become. I want you to take the road less traveled to become more of who you are. For the next few chapters, ignore the societal pressures that tell you to conform and assimilate, to make your weaknesses your strengths, or to become someone else. In certain corporate cultures, the pressure for sameness can be very high—even demanded. If we mimic the behaviors we've witnessed from other leaders, especially those who lead in unsavory ways, we become exactly the person we've hated working for and have never wanted to be. The relentless pressure to conform is like a flood-stage river, swallowing up everything in its path. It is unyielding, and we all can get carried away.

What Harm Could a Balloon Do?

The truth is that we hear this story repeatedly: leaders are thrown into the role with little to no training. It happened to me. One day, I was an individual contributor; the next, I had a leadership title—no training, guidance, or road map. Not even a desk. Our company was growing fast and space was limited, so I had to set up at the same desk as my former manager, someone I admired and had learned a lot from. That proximity ended up being a gift, as it allowed me to ask a lot of questions and observe his leadership up close.

Having a good role model helped, but it didn't mean I always got it right. My results would let me know loud and clear whenever I didn't. For example, I found an idea in a book about how to motivate your team by creating clear and visible accountability. I ran with it. I bought helium balloons and tied one to each person's chair. The deal? Hit your sales goal, pop the balloon, win a prize.

What could go wrong? Turns out, plenty!

Ultimately, only three people hit the goal. The rest sat awkwardly, their balloons floating above them like a shameful public scoreboard. Even the ones who'd popped their balloons hated this idea I'd implemented. I hadn't realized how humiliating or divisive it would feel. That well-intentioned idea? Straight to the trash—along with the balloon scraps.

It was a humbling wake-up call. If I wanted to lead well, I had to start by knowing who I needed to be. That moment marked the beginning of my journey toward oneness.

Self-Awareness

After working with countless leaders over the years, I've spotted some interesting patterns. Some habits serve leaders really well, while others . . . not so much. One that keeps coming up has to do with a massive gap in self-awareness. For example, when I ask leaders how they think they're doing, the vast majority will say above average. But when I ask their employees to rate those same leaders, very few see it the same way.

Behind this is a lack of self-awareness, absence of needed feedback, unclear expectations, and something called the "fundamental attribution error," wherein we tend to judge others by their flaws and ourselves by our intentions. Leaders overestimate their effectiveness, whereas employees see the reality.

To bridge this gap, leaders must own their shortcomings, ask for feedback, and commit to growth. When teams see leaders doing that—being honest, vulnerable, and coachable—they give grace. But if they sense ego and defensiveness, engagement drops, performance suffers, and turnover rises.

Self-awareness isn't innate; it's a skill you can build. We recognize it in others, but it's harder to see in ourselves. Two proven tools to enhance your self-awareness are reflection and feedback. They fuel metacognition—our ability to observe and adjust our own behavior— which is the key to conscious leadership. The more you practice it, the stronger and more authentic your leadership becomes.

Now layer on the pressure to conform.

Corporate cultures often push for compliance, sameness, and assimilation. We admire bold, authentic leadership yet so often reward imitation. Many leaders end up emulating someone else—sometimes even a person who's exhibiting the very behavior they once vowed to avoid.

But why? Because we don't train leaders properly. The Center for Creative Leadership found that 60 percent of first-time managers receive no formal leadership training.[ii] None. Instead, many mimic the loudest voice in the room, even if that voice leads through fear, bravado, or a "leave a trail of dead bodies" attitude.

Let's be clear: fear-based leadership is not real leadership. And if that's your thing, this book may not be for you.

Why don't we do a better job of setting people up for success? One of the big challenges is the belief that success in the role of individual contributor will lead to success in leadership. What is right about this thinking is that someone might know how to do the job, has demonstrated success, and has shown a high level of performance. But what's wrong with this is that the skills required to be a leader are different from those of an individual contributor; the focus goes from "me" to "we"—and that is a big shift. Emotional intelligence is critical in leadership, and not everyone has developed it—empowering and delegating are not easy skills to acquire. Finally, it's hard to make the shift, and many new leaders get very frustrated because they are used to being successful, and their frustration or negativity could impact the team.

Let's look at it another way: what if we hired pilots to fly planes with little to no training? Promoting untrained leaders is no different; it would be like putting a pilot in the cockpit only after having watched the film *Top Gun*: dangerous and disorienting. But isn't this practically the same thing we do to our employees? We promote wildly unprepared leaders—no training, no guidance, and often not even a book under their belt. And though most businesses don't deal in life-or-death decisions, poor leadership still leaves casualties.

Disengagement. Burnout. Turnover. Missed targets. Stalled growth. And the damage doesn't stop at the office door—it follows people home, impacting their mental health, their families, and even their futures. That's the cost of putting unprepared leaders in charge. And it's why the world doesn't just need more leaders; it needs better ones. It starts with you.

But here's the real problem: too many leaders are told to "do what I did." So they fake it. They copy someone else's style, tone, and presence, thinking that's what leadership is. But when you lead like someone you're not, it doesn't just feel wrong; it looks wrong. People may not say it out loud, but they feel it. And they don't follow leaders they can't trust.

Leadership isn't cosplay. It's not a role you take on. If the playbook you've been given doesn't make space for the real you, burn it. You weren't made to mimic. You were made to lead—with courage, clarity, and your own voice.

Take Patrick Mahomes and Andy Reid of the Kansas City Chiefs. Three Super Bowl wins in five years, a team-record 15-2 season, and nearly achieving a first-ever NFL championship three-peat in 2025. They've built a dynasty—not just on talent but also trust.

Reid sets the strategy. Mahomes brings it to life with instinct and improvisation. Reid doesn't micromanage. Mahomes doesn't just execute—he leads. That balance is what makes them unstoppable.

That's the kind of leadership we're aiming for. This book gives you the what. The how? That's on you. Bring your instincts. Bring your voice. Bring your brilliance.

Because leadership isn't about copying the playbook—it's about owning the field.

My passion for empowering BOLD leaders comes from our need to have more great leaders in the world who are the best version of their true selves to make a positive impact. Leaders create a big impact followed by a ripple effect and have the opportunity to lift everyone up around them.

Going back to the example of the impacts of poor leadership, in contrast, BOLD leaders create a ripple effect of engagement, efficiency, and growth, elevating both team performance and organizational success. Beyond the workplace, their positive influence fosters well-being and harmony in personal and family dynamics, emphasizing the value of empathy, emotional intelligence, and balance. BOLD leadership inspires not only results but also a healthier, more connected world—starting with you.

This is the time to ask yourself what kind of leader you want to be. Since your power comes from what comes naturally, in this phase of the BOLD leadership journey, we uncover your true, authentic self—and that power fuels your strong leadership. Creating a BOLD and powerful you is best started by focusing on four areas: foundation, future vision, truth, and growth. Foundation is getting clear on where you are right now—the good, the bad, and the ugly—clarity on what matters to you and why and how you want that to play out in your life. Let's begin there.

Getting Clear on Who You Are

The first step to becoming a BOLD leader is developing deep self-awareness. That starts with taking honest stock of where you are right now.

Expert tip: as no single assessment can define you, using a mix of tools gives you a more complete picture—highlighting the strengths you can leverage and the patterns that may be holding you back.

Define Your Purpose, Values, and Vision

When you know your why, your work moves from your head to your heart. That clarity fuels meaning, motivation, and momentum. What drives you to lead? What kind of impact do you want to make? What values will guide your decisions?

Here's a sample purpose statement to inspire your own:

My purpose as a leader is to inspire and empower individuals to reach their full potential. I strive to build a culture of trust, respect, and collaboration where people feel valued and supported to learn, innovate, and excel.

And what about values? Your values shape how you show up every day. Consider these real-life examples:

- Jacinda Ardern (former prime minister of New Zealand): empathy, inclusivity, transparency
- Ruth Bader Ginsburg (US Supreme Court 1993–2020): justice, wisdom, advocacy
- Satya Nadella (CEO of Microsoft Corporation): growth, accountability, empathy

Reflect on what matters most to you—and how you want those values to show up in your leadership.

Use Tools to Deepen Self-Awareness

Once you've grounded yourself in purpose and values, assessments can help you go deeper. Our favorites include:

- Gallup CliftonStrengths (top pick): Uncovers your natural talents to develop into exponential strengths
- Kolbe, DISC, and Myers–Briggs Type Indicator (MBTI): Helps illuminate how you take action, make decisions, and interact with others

No assessment tells the whole story, but together, they offer powerful insights.

Ask for Feedback—Even When It's Difficult

Feedback is your leadership mirror. Don't just wait for it—go seek it out. Ask your manager, peers, direct reports, clients, and/or vendors for honest input on your strengths and areas for growth.

Try asking:

- "How would you describe me to someone who doesn't know me?"
- "What's something I should do more of? Less of?"

And when you hear something that stings, don't argue. Just say, "Thank you." Then look for the patterns—what shows up consistently is likely your reality.

I know this firsthand. Early in my leadership journey, I thought I was doing great. But my peers didn't agree—and they weren't wrong. I was isolating myself, thinking I didn't need their support. But the truth is that this mindset was holding me back. It wasn't until I started listening, opening up, and seeking feedback that I really began to grow.

Go Deeper with a 360

One of the most powerful tools I've seen is the 360 assessment. We use it often with clients, and it can be humbling—but also transformational. It's not always easy to hear how others experience you, especially when your self-perception doesn't match. But that contrast is where growth begins.

When we stop flying blind and start listening with openness, we begin to see what's been getting in our way—and we gain the clarity to lead with confidence, authenticity, and impact.

Align with Your Integrity: Who Do You Want to Be?

Integrity is often defined as honesty or doing the right thing when no one's watching—and that's true. But at its core, integrity is about wholeness. It's being fully yourself and staying true to what you believe, even when it's inconvenient or unpopular. The more energy you spend trying to be who others expect you to be, the less you have to lead with clarity and conviction.

Warren Buffett put it simply: "If you're not sure whether something is right or wrong, consider whether you'd be OK with it showing up in the morning paper."

An executive coach once shared a version I'll never forget: "If your words or actions were featured on *60 Minutes*, would you be proud?"

We've all regretted those moments when we ignored our inner "spidey sense" that told us, "This isn't right." The more we tune into that voice, the more we lead with integrity—and the less likely we are to land ourselves in the leadership penalty box.

There's a story about Mahatma Gandhi that captures this beautifully. A mother once waited in line with her son to ask him to tell the boy to stop eating sugar, as it was harming his health. Gandhi told them to come back in three weeks. When they returned, he looked the boy in the eye and said, "You must stop eating sugar." The boy agreed. The mother, confused, asked why Gandhi hadn't just said that earlier.

He replied, "Because I was still eating sugar."

Powerful. Gandhi wouldn't ask someone to do something he wasn't willing to do himself. That's integrity in action.

So here's the question I'll leave you with: where in your life are you saying one thing but doing another?

Identify those gaps. Then take one step—just one—to close the distance between your actions and your values. You don't have to overhaul everything overnight. Progress is made in small, consistent steps.

BOLD leaders don't lead perfectly. But they lead honestly. They align their actions with their values, their voice with their truth, and their leadership with who they really are.

That's the power of oneness. That's BOLD!

BOLD Takeaways

- **Be you, not them.** Your greatest power comes from leading as your true self—not as a copy of someone else.

- **Know yourself so you can lead yourself.** Self-awareness is the foundation of BOLD leadership. Build it through reflection and feedback.

- **Burn that wrong playbook.** If the leadership style you're copying doesn't fit, ditch it. Lead with your own voice.

- **Integrity is alignment.** Say what you mean. Do what you say. Close the gap—consistently.

Chapter 4:
A Self-Awareness & Integrity Deep-Dive Exercise for BOLD Leaders

Step 1: Assess—Gain Clarity on Where You Are Right Now

Becoming a BOLD leader starts with self-awareness. Before you can lead others well, you need to understand who you are, what drives you, and how others experience you.

Start here:

Define Your Purpose, Values, and Vision

Your Purpose Statement

This is your why—your personal North Star as a leader. It captures your deepest motivations, your intended impact, and who you aspire to be.

Reflect and Journal

- What is the deeper reason I choose to lead?
- What impact do I want to make?
- What drives me—especially in hard times?
- What kind of culture or experience do I want to create?

Once you've explored these questions, craft your personal leadership purpose statement. Remember: done is better than perfect. Revisit and revise as you grow.

Example Purpose Statement

My purpose as a leader is to inspire and empower others to reach their full potential by fostering a culture of trust, respect, and growth.

Your Values

These are your inner compass—how you lead. What principles shape your decisions and define your leadership?

Examples: empathy, curiosity, innovation, accountability, courage, justice, service

Reflect and Write
- Which three to five values matter most to me?
- When I'm at my best, which values am I honoring?
- What happens when I stray from them?

Inspiration
- **Jacinda Ardern:** empathy, inclusivity
- **Ruth Bader Ginsburg:** justice, perseverance
- **Satya Nadella:** growth, empathy, innovation

Use Assessments to Deepen Your Understanding
No single tool tells the whole story, but a few good ones offer powerful insights.
Our favorites:
- **CliftonStrengths (Gallup):** best for uncovering your natural talents
- **Kolbe, DISC, MBTI:** great for understanding how you take action, interact, and make decisions

Gather Feedback (Yes, Even the Tough Stuff)
Ask people who know you well—your boss, peers, team, clients:

"What's one thing I do well—and one thing I should do differently?"
Look for patterns. Be open. Resist the urge to defend. The goal is not perfection—it's progress.

Try this prompt:
- "How would you describe me to someone who doesn't know me?"
- "What's something I should do more of? Less of?"

Once you receive the feedback, say, "Thank you." That's it. No excuses, no explanations.

Reflect
Set aside quiet time and ask yourself:
- "What feedback resonates most?"
- "What surprised me?"
- "What do I want to change or do differently?"

- "Am I showing up in alignment with my purpose and values?"
- "How do I want to be remembered as a leader?"

Step 2: Align—with Integrity

Integrity isn't just about honesty; it's about wholeness. Are you living and leading in alignment with who you truly are?
Ask yourself:

- "Where in my leadership am I saying one thing but doing another?"
- "What would I not want to see about me on the front page of the newspaper?"
- "Where do I need to realign with my values or purpose?"

Guiding Insight from Warren Buffett:
"If you wouldn't be proud to see it in the morning paper, don't do it."

And from Gandhi:
Only after he stopped eating sugar himself did he tell a boy to do the same. Lead by example. Always.

Final Reflection:
What's one small action you can take today to close the gap between how you're showing up and who you want to be?
Write it down. Then do it. BOLDly.

Chapter 5

Become the Leader You're Meant to Be

"The best way to predict the future is to create it."
—Peter Drucker

You would be shocked by the number of leaders who have zero plans for their career and development. They have simply taken paths that others have led them to. This might be you. All of us are likely guilty of putting our heads down and from time to time just forging ahead without thinking about where we will end up. As you look up, you think, Where am I? Take a step back and rise above the fray to identify and claim your future self. Be the leader you really want to be.

Like we did in the Brilliant Vision section for our company and/or our teams, now is the time to define the brilliant vision for you. How do you want to lead? Take a step back and get clear on who you want to be. What is the impact you want to make in the world and on those around you? What is your purpose? Clearly defining it will help keep you on the right path on your journey.

Defining Your Future Self

The psychological research on the future self examines the processes and consequences associated with thinking about oneself in the future. People think about their future selves in a similar way to how they think about others.[iii] How connected people feel to their future selves—whether through similarity, closeness, or identification—affects how thoughtfully they treat that future version of themselves.[iv] When you feel close to your future self, you're more likely to make choices today that set you up for success tomorrow—like saving money, staying healthy, and doing the right thing. Simple shifts that boost that connection can lead to smarter, more future-focused decisions.[v]

What Happens If We Don't Have a Vision for Our Future Self?

Failure to plan could mean your future self won't achieve the goal or that you will only achieve in some areas. Life could be out of balance; you give everything to your business but your family doesn't really know you or, worse, actually hates you. You have no friends; you're not taking care of your health; you aren't sleeping or eating right. This can have drastic effects on your ability to work, as well as your longevity.

Our actions have a cumulative effect when we don't take care of ourselves—and will not result in our reaching our desired future self. In contrast, if we care for ourselves, then our quality of life will be better, and our longevity likely will as well.

How can we plan for the days leading to the future self we want to become?

Out of sight, out of mind. There's a danger in long-term planning being out of sight and then leading to being out of mind. Such planning will hit you later, and you'll eventually say, "Oh yeah, I should get back into that." Stay on track by keeping the vision of your future self in front of you. The silver lining is that these unforeseen events can be a wake-up call for you to get on the path to the future self you want to be.

Lost in the Forest?

Sometimes, we can't see the forest for the trees—we get so caught up in the moment that we lose sight of the bigger picture. But once you have a clear sense of who you are, you'll be ready to envision the future you're meant to create.

If you were leading at your BOLDest, what would that look like? If you saw leadership as the incredible adventure it truly is, who could you become?

Here's how to begin:

1. **Reflect.** Look back on your past moments of courage—the times you took the road less traveled, even when it was hard. When were you called to be bold, courageous, or fearless? What was the situation? How did you navigate it? What actions did you take? What did you look and feel like at your bravest? How did it feel to make it through?

2. **Study.** Identify the leaders you admire most—those who embody boldness and adventure. Who inspires you? Whom would you love to emulate? Go on a role-model journey: research them, learn their stories, and create a list of the leaders who light a fire in you.

Self-Awareness Leads to Strength

One of my most admired friends from college, Willie Barney, is a true example of authentic, BOLD leadership. Willie, along with his wife, Yolanda, has dedicated his life to creating real change—and his journey will inspire you as much as it inspires me.

Willie grew up in rural Mississippi, witnessing firsthand the lasting impacts of poverty, segregation, and injustice on communities of color. But, his family maintained high expectations. Later, as he traveled the country for work as a successful marketer at a Midwest-based media company, he saw these patterns repeating across the US. It stirred something deeper within him—a calling he couldn't ignore. After careful reflection, Willie made the courageous decision to leave his corporate career and launch the Empowerment Network, an organization focused on addressing systemic challenges in the Black community of Omaha, Nebraska.

During a conversation, Willie shared that when he first completed his CliftonStrengths assessment, he was excited to see the results but found one thing discouraging. Empathy didn't show up as one of his top strengths, and at first, it shook his confidence. But as we explored his results more deeply, he realized something powerful: Willie's strengths in strategy and individualization were the BOLD leadership traits that made him so effective. His ability to see the big picture and tailor solutions to individuals' unique talents and needs was precisely what his mission required. This deeper self-awareness combined with reflection helped him not only accept but celebrate his authentic leadership style—allowing him to lean even more fully into his work.

The results speak for themselves. Willie has stepped into his purpose to unite leaders across sectors in Omaha, focusing on the upstream issues of unemployment, education, housing, entrepreneurship, and poverty. Every week for one hour, these leaders come together to identify specific actions and follow through. Nineteen years later, through extensive collaboration, gun violence has dropped by 80 percent, graduation rates have soared from 50 percent to 81 percent, and unemployment has fallen from 21 percent to just 7 percent. His BOLD leadership has created ripples far beyond Omaha—he's been honored by the Obama Foundation, featured on CNN and CBS, and now mentors 13 cities nationwide seeking to replicate his model. His God-given vision has touched thousands of lives locally and impacted a city of a million people and communities across the nation.

That's what happens when leaders lead with authenticity, self-awareness, and purpose.

That's BOLD.

Greatest Hits of Leadership

A helpful way to create your vision for success is to think of leaders you admire. There are many places to learn about inspiring leadership and to create your vision: leaders you interact with, great books, podcasts, blogs, and magazines such as Harvard Business Review. Assemble your own "best of" list and intentionally invest time and create a plan to refine your skills and utilize the practices you admire most. Adapt what you learn to fit your goals.

Who are your leadership role models?

When I think about truly BOLD leaders who lead with self-awareness and authenticity, five names stand out: Mary Dillon, Mary Barra, Nelson

Mandela, Satya Nadella, and Jacinda Ardern. Each of them embodies the courage to lead in their own way, staying grounded in their values while inspiring transformational change. Mary Dillon built thriving cultures at such Fortune 500 firms as Foot Locker, Ulta Beauty, McDonald's, and UScellular by blending business success with deep care for people. Mary Barra leads one of the world's largest companies—General Motors— with transparency, resilience, and a relentless focus on innovation. The late Nelson Mandela, erstwhile president of South Africa, modeled forgiveness and integrity, showing that true strength comes from leading with purpose and heart. Satya Nadella transformed Microsoft's culture as CEO by putting empathy and learning at the center of leadership. And former New Zealand prime minister Jacinda Ardern brought compassion and authenticity to global leadership, proving that kindness and strength are not mutually exclusive. These leaders remind us that the most powerful leadership isn't about perfection—it's about knowing who you are, staying true to it, and boldly bringing others along with you.

Early in my leadership journey, I dove into such books as *The One Minute Manager*, *Raving Fans*, *Who Moved My Cheese?*, and others. They gave me simple but powerful strategies: set clear goals, celebrate progress, guide people through change, deliver exceptional customer experiences, and coach others to grow. These ideas gave me tools I could immediately use while helping me stay true to the leader I wanted to become. As I grew, I kept learning, exploring deeper leadership insights from other books such as *The Leadership Challenge, Multipliers, and Mindset*. The truth is that leadership isn't something you master once; it's a lifelong adventure. Pick a topic you're curious about, dig into great resources—books, TED Talks, articles, podcasts— and then take what resonates and make it your own. The best leaders are always learning, growing, and leading from a place that's uniquely theirs. Study great leaders. Then do you.

Claiming Your Future Self

At the end of this chapter, you'll find the Perfect Day Exercise—your chance to create a BOLD vision and ignite the journey to both becoming the leader and living the life you dream of.

Expert tip: Your future self starts with vision. Picture that version of yourself vividly. Who are you? What impact are you making? How does it feel to live fully aligned with your purpose?

The clearer your vision, the faster you'll move toward it—and the more unstoppable you'll become. I believe that my future self continues to evolve to this day. It started with the first time I ever committed it to paper when I was working with a career coach who told me, "Write down what your future self is like. What is she doing? Where is she living? What is her life like?"

I'd never thought like that about where I wanted to be. I always wanted to improve, do better, grow, and achieve at the next level. That was always in my mind. But having a vision of what my life would be had never happened before. If I could design any life that I wanted, what life would that be?

First, I thought about what I already had:

- A wonderful husband who loves me? Check.
- Great kids I have strong relationships with? Check.
- Enriching relationships with family and friends? Check.
- Generous and wise mentors? Check.
- Experience? Check.

I decided to dream big and cast a vision of my family and me living in Hawaii. Why not live in one of my favorite places in the world? What would I need in order to achieve that vision as my future self? How did my current life mesh with that? Here's what I came up with:

- I saw myself running a business that I loved, where I was consulting and spending time helping leaders achieve their most important goals. Thinking about the value I would bring to my clients was exciting and invigorating.
- Nonprofit endeavors that were meaningful and mattered a great deal to me were integrated into my business.
- I envisioned my workspace to be indoor/outdoor. After all, I love being outdoors. You could have meetings inside or outside. Typically, office buildings don't have any fresh air coming in, which is something that's always bothered me.

- I pictured our family living in an old farmhouse in Hawaii with big verandas around the outside. It would be nestled on a hill with beautiful ocean views and nice breezes. We would have horses for my girls and dogs for me.

As I started to put these elements in place, I found myself getting clearer with each detail. I can still picture it right now. I'm not living in Hawaii—as I reevaluated and realized that I would miss being close to my friends and extended family—but most everything else in my plan has come true or is in the process of being so. After all, Hawaii will always be there to visit.

Mapping the Perfect Day

Once you have determined what some of those key elements for your future self are, the next step is to map out what your future self's "perfect day" might look like. What would happen on that day for you?

For me, once I'd envisioned my life in Hawaii with my family, mapping out my perfect day looked like this:

- Wake up and go for a run.
- Walk the dogs.
- Make sure the kids are up for school.
- Ensure that everybody eats breakfast together.
- Go to my home office and start my day by making a few phone calls.
- Go to an office I have in town and spend my day meeting with my team and clients, creating value and making an impact.
- Spend lunchtime with someone interested in the nonprofit side of our business whom I am looking to potentially partner with.
- Work until 3 p.m., then cut out of the office to meet my husband.
- We pick our kids up from school and then head to the beach, where we surf for the next couple hours together as a family, having a blast. (DREAM BIG!)
- After surfing, we head to a private beach club that we belong to, change, and go to the restaurant there for dinner. Everybody there knows us, and it feels like family.
- We go back home, where the girls do their homework, I have a little bit of work to do, and my husband does too.

- At night, I'm packing my suitcase because I'm getting ready to head out on a trip the next day to go to Indonesia (haven't been there yet—new country).
- I wrap up the night by sitting outside with my husband, right by our outdoor fireplace, enjoying the evening and having a little quiet time before going to bed.

BOLD leadership doesn't happen by accident; it starts with vision. In this chapter, you explored the power of intentionally shaping your future self and your leadership journey. Without a clear vision, it's easy to drift, letting others chart your course. But when you reflect on your authentic strengths, study bold role models, and imagine the leader you want to become, you create a road map to a future filled with purpose, impact, and meaning. Your future self isn't just a dream—it's a destination you build with every decision you make today. By envisioning your BOLD future and mapping your perfect day, you take ownership of your path, step into your full potential, and lead the adventure of your life.

BOLD Takeaways

- **Own your future.** You can't create the life and leadership you want without a clear vision—define it now before someone else does it for you.

- **Reflect on your best moments.** Look back at when you've already been the best of yourself—when you have lived up to the vision you have of your leadership. These are the clues to who you are at your best.

- **Learn from bold leaders.** Study the leaders who inspire you most—not to copy them but to find inspiration to craft your own authentic style.

- **Design your future self.** The clearer you are about who you want to become, the more powerful your actions today will be in bringing that vision to life.

Chapter 5:
Perfect Day Exercise

In this exercise, you will create a detailed journal entry about your perfect day. For 24 hours, you get to do exactly what you want; make the impact, live your purpose fully from start to finish.

Now it's your turn. Let's create your perfect day. Tell me about it.

What does the perfect day look like for you? Where are you? What's happening? What are the sounds, tastes, and smells around you?

Close your eyes. Picture it. Go online and find images that capture it to create a vision board.

A vision board is a tool that helps you keep your goals in front of you. The idea behind it is simple: whatever your mind can envision, you can achieve. Find visuals/pictures that represent your goals.

Be detailed, visualize it first in your mind, and then capture it in your journal entry. Go somewhere that is inspiring to you and distraction-free. Allow yourself time to think and dream. A way to organize your vision is to answer the following: who, what, when, where, and how?

All those items on your board can contribute to you leading a great life as you define it. Make time and space to think about what you really want. These ideas are inside of you; you're probably just not giving yourself the time to listen to them.

Here Are Some More-Detailed Questions to Get You Started:

- Where do you wake up? If not at home, where?
- What time do you wake up?
- Do you have a morning routine? If so, what does it consist of?
- What types of activities do you partake in throughout the day? How long are you spending on each activity?
- What is the weather like?
- Where are you spending your time?
- Who is with you?

- What are you doing?
- What is your work and how do you do it?
- How do you integrate your business and your lifestyle?
- How is your balance of work/personal/family?
- How do you fit your long-range goals with your short-term needs?
- What aren't you doing?
- How do you feel?
- What do you eat and drink throughout the day? Where do you eat and drink? Are you alone or with other people?
- Do you exercise? If so, what type and for how long?
- Do you see anyone else that day? If so, who? What do you do together?
- Do you have an evening routine? If so, what does it consist of?
- What time do you go to bed?
- How do you feel as you end your day?

Frequently Asked Questions About the Perfect Day Exercise

1. How often should I do this exercise?

Your perfect day will change over time. This isn't a "do it once and never do it again" activity. You should aim to review it once a year and refine as needed.

2. What tense should I write in?

Write your perfect day in the present tense as if it is happening in that very moment.

3. How far into the future should I set my perfect day?

Imagine your perfect day 5 years from now. And after you've done 5 years a few times, try different lengths of time, such as 1 to 10 years and beyond.

4. What should I do once I've written out the exercise?

Add the date to the exercise so you know when you wrote it. This is especially useful if you keep the exercise and look back at it in the future. Then come back to the exercise a few days later and compare your ideal day to your written goals and/or your vision board.

Chapter 5, Exercise 2:
Define Your Leadership Vision Statement

A vision statement is a concise and aspirational statement that describes a leader's long-term goals and aspirations. It is future oriented and is focused on what a leader wants in order to achieve and where they are going.

Here's an example of my leadership vision statement:

My vision as a leader is to empower my team to consistently exceed goals, deliver transformative results for our customers and stakeholders, and set a new standard of excellence that inspires positive change across our industry and the world.

What steps should you take to create your own leadership vision statement? Start by reflecting on powerful questions.

Here Are a Few to Guide You as You Define Your Leadership Vision:

- What kind of culture or environment do I want to create as a leader?
- What long-term goals or legacy do I aspire to achieve?
- When my leadership journey is over, how do I want to be remembered by my team, organization, and community?
- What stories or achievements would I like others to tell about my leadership?
- How will my leadership have shaped the careers, lives, or personal growth of those I've led?
- What lasting changes or systems do I want to implement to benefit future leaders or teams?
- How can I ensure that my leadership legacy aligns with my values and purpose?
- What would my team, peers, and stakeholders say about me if they were writing my leadership "biography" today?
- How can I create a sustainable impact that outlasts my time in my role and/or organization?

- What will my leadership mean to the people beyond my immediate circle (e.g., families, communities, society)?

Again, give yourself some quiet time and journal your answers. You can then utilize your answers to craft your leadership vision statement. Just like the purpose statement, done is better than perfect, and you can revise it as often as you would like.

Chapter 6

Close the Gap

"You don't make progress by standing on the sidelines, whimpering and complaining. You make progress by implementing ideas."
—Shirley Chisholm

You need a plan to get from where you are today to where you want to be. My first piece of advice? Take it one step at a time. Trying to change everything at once is overwhelming and almost always leads to frustration or burnout. Instead, start small, stay focused, and build momentum.

Look at the key areas that would make the biggest difference for you. What skills, habits, or mindsets could you strengthen that would have the greatest impact? Focus on a few meaningful changes, not everything all at once. You can use tools such as setting SMART (specific, measurable, achievable, relevant, and time-bound) goals, building a simple road map, or working backward from your vision to identify your next right steps.

Think about the easiest wins—the small shifts that could create big results. Maybe it's improving how you delegate, building stronger relationships, or setting clearer priorities. Then take intentional action: read a book, watch a TED Talk, practice a new behavior, or ask for feedback. Progress happens when you focus your energy on what matters most and keep moving forward, one bold step at a time.

If you're ready to double down on building your future one bold step at a time, check out *The Compound Effect* by Darren Hardy, *Atomic*

Habits by James Clear, *Grit* by Angela Duckworth, and *Essentialism* by Greg McKeown.[vi] These books all deliver the same powerful truth: success isn't about giant leaps; it's about small moves made consistently with focus and determination. You don't have to overhaul your life overnight. Start where you are, take the next right step, and stay with it. That's how BOLD leaders are made—one courageous, committed action at a time.

Mary Barra's Bold Journey from Here to There

Mary Barra, the first female CEO of General Motors (GM), has exemplified bold and transformative leadership by taking the automotive giant from its traditional roots to the forefront of electric mobility. When Barra took the helm in 2014, GM was still heavily reliant on gas-powered vehicles and grappling with the aftermath of a major recall scandal. Despite these challenges, she saw an opportunity to redefine GM's legacy by pivoting toward a sustainable and innovative future. Her bold vision for a "zero crashes, zero emissions, zero congestion" world became the guiding principle for GM's transformation.

To get there, she did the following:

1. **Set clear goals.** Barra made it clear that GM's future lay in electric vehicles (EVs), stating publicly that GM would phase out gas-powered vehicles entirely by 2035. This was no small ambition for a company deeply entrenched in producing combustion engines. In 2021, she set SMART goals, such as investing $35 billion in EV and autonomous-vehicle development by 2025 and launching 30 new EV models worldwide within the same timeframe. This road map was designed to position GM as a leader in the competitive EV market while signaling a strong commitment to sustainability.
2. **Built a road map.** Barra's plan to achieve this bold vision was both strategic and actionable.
3. **Prioritized.**

a. **Investment in technology.** GM poured billions into EV battery development, including creating the Ultium Platform, a modular battery system designed for scalability and efficiency across a range of vehicles.

b. **Partnerships and collaboration.** GM partnered with companies such as Honda and LG Chem to accelerate innovation and reduce costs, ensuring that EVs would be accessible to a broader market.

c. **Cultural shift.** Barra knew that transforming GM's product lineup required transforming its culture. She encouraged a more inclusive and innovative workplace, where employees felt empowered to contribute to the company's bold new direction.

d. **Customer focus.** Recognizing the importance of consumer adoption, GM launched campaigns to educate the public about EV benefits and address such common concerns as charging infrastructure and affordability.

4. **Executed the vision.** Barra's leadership was not just about setting goals; it was about relentlessly pursuing them. Under her watch, GM introduced groundbreaking models such as the all-electric Chevrolet Bolt and, more recently, the Cadillac Lyriq and GMC Hummer EV. These vehicles have redefined GM's brand and made electric mobility exciting and aspirational.

5. **Saw results and recognition.** The results of Barra's vision and road map are already evident as GM has emerged as a leader in the EV space, competing head-to-head with Tesla and other innovators. By committing to a clear vision and building a robust plan to get there, Barra has positioned GM as not only a leader in sustainability but also a company capable of reinventing itself for the future.

Leaders Are Learners

BOLD leaders understand an essential truth: to lead others, you must first lead yourself.

That means committing to constant learning, growth, and evolution—closing your own gaps so you can help others close theirs.

Great leaders aren't fearless; they feel fear and move forward anyway. They lean into uncertainty. They explore the uncharted. And they never believe they've "arrived."

Regardless of experience, role, or the stage of the journey, the best leaders are lifelong learners.

Whether it's through books (yes, real ones, with pages), webinars, mentors, experiences, or even observing both great and poor role models, BOLD leaders are always seeking knowledge. They know that growth isn't optional; it's essential for building resourcefulness, confidence, and resilience. Learning equips us to light the way for others. It transforms uncharted territory into navigable ground.

Learning Through Mistakes

I learned this lesson the hard way early in my career. After moving into an operations role to help fix customer issues, I believed that my sales experience had given me all the answers. In one of my first meetings, when a teammate proposed a new centralized system, I immediately shot the idea down without truly listening. I thought I was helping. Instead, I came across as a condescending know-it-all.

Later, a brave colleague pulled me aside and told me how my behavior had been received. It was painful to hear—but exactly what I needed. I realized that I hadn't partnered with the team, hadn't asked for more context, and hadn't listened before speaking. I needed to learn more before weighing in, but I had come into this new role with the attitude that I already knew all I needed to know. I couldn't undo the damage, but I could change how I would show up moving forward.

That feedback sparked a major growth moment—and a lifelong commitment to learning to lead better by listening and learning.

As leaders rise, honest feedback becomes harder to come by. We must stay humble, stay curious, and stay willing to learn—from anyone. Continuous learning matters. The pace of change in business today is exponential. In our capitalist economy, the expectation of constant improvement is both a blessing and a challenge. It demands agility. It demands that we stay sharp, resilient, and open.

I've worked for organizations where "heart-attack quarters"—sprinting every 90 days—were the norm. It was exciting but exhausting. The reality is that what worked yesterday won't necessarily work tomorrow. Those who keep learning will keep leading. Those who don't will fall behind.

Look around—there are examples everywhere:

- AI is transforming business models overnight.
- Uber redefined transportation—and challenged decades-old industries.
- Zoom became essential almost instantly when the world shifted during COVID-19.

The technology itself isn't the biggest story. The willingness to learn and adapt is.

Lighthouse leaders don't fear change—they embrace it. They know that by continuously learning, they can confidently step into the unknown, lighting the way for others to follow.

Build the Plan

Building a developmental plan is a powerful way to move you forward from where you are to where you want to be. Consider the following questions:

- What do you want to keep and what do you want to change?
- How will you measure success?
- How will you know when you have achieved the goal of your best future self?
- Whom will you ask for help?

BOLD leaders apply the SMART framework with a focus on personal growth, team impact, and innovation. A SMART goal is a structured way of setting objectives to ensure that they are actionable, measurable, and aligned with your personal and professional growth. SMART stands for specific, measurable, achievable, relevant, and time-bound:

- **Specific.** Clearly define what you want to achieve.
  Example: "Improve my emotional intelligence by actively listening during team meetings."
- **Measurable.** Establish how success will be measured.
  Example: "Increase my team's feedback rating on my listening skills from 3.5 to 4.5 on a 5-point scale within six months."
- **Achievable.** Ensure that the goal is realistic and attainable.
  Example: "Spend 15 minutes daily reflecting on interactions to identify patterns in my communication style."
- **Relevant.** Make sure your goal aligns with your long-term leadership vision.
  Example: "Enhance my emotional intelligence to foster better team collaboration and trust."
- **Time-Bound.** Set a clear deadline.
  Example: "Complete an emotional-intelligence workshop and practice learned techniques by the end of the next quarter."

Here are the steps to take to create your SMART goals:

Step 1: Identify the goals you want to achieve. For example, I want to empower my team by asking more questions, becoming a better listener, and allowing them to own their work and solve their own problems, all while being a supportive leader.

Step 2: Set the KPIs. For example:
- The number of questions asked
- Question-to-answer ratio
- Fewer questions coming to you
- Feedback from those you interact with regularly

Step 3: Select the actions you will take. For example, prepare ahead of meetings by thinking about the questions you will ask. Research powerful questions and add new ones to your list. Bring something to each meeting to capture responses. If you are taking careful notes, it's less likely you will interrupt or do too much talking.

Step 4: Enlist help. For example, ask a trusted colleague or two to monitor your question/answer ratio and provide you with feedback.

Documenting your development plan is crucial because it turns ideas into actionable steps, making your vision tangible and achievable. Writing down your plan helps clarify your goals, organize your thoughts, and track your progress. It serves as a road map, ensuring that you stay focused and aligned with your long-term aspirations.

Expert tip: sharing your documented plan with others provides accountability, as it invites feedback, support, and encouragement from peers, mentors, and/or coaches.

This level of commitment increases the likelihood of follow-through and helps you navigate challenges with greater confidence and support. A documented plan isn't just a tool for growth; it's a statement of intention and a commitment to achieving your leadership potential.

What Might Get in the Way?

Even with a clear vision and strong intentions, obstacles will show up—they always do. The good news? Most of what gets in the way isn't out there. It's inside: self-doubt, fear, and the pressure to be someone you're not. Recognizing these roadblocks is the first step to overcoming them. If you know what might trip you up, you can face it head-on and keep moving boldly toward your future.

Here are a few of the biggest challenges to watch for:

- **Negative Self Talk**

  Our ego often masquerades as a source of confidence, but more often it's a voice of fear—afraid of getting bruised or hurt. It talks us out of taking the leaps that could change everything. "Who am I to do this? Who would believe in me?" In these moments, we become our own worst enemy. Sometimes, it's not even our own fear we're hearing; it's the fear of others. "I could never do that." (Yes, you can!)

When I think about moments when I stepped up—such as presenting a compelling story to an executive committee—I remember the energy, the connection, the sense of "I'm meant to be here." Had I let fear or self-doubt win, I would have missed those peak experiences that shaped my growth.

- **Imposter Syndrome**

  This affects more leaders than you might think. It's not just a "women's issue"—it impacts everyone at some point. Imposter syndrome makes accomplished, capable people convince themselves that they don't deserve their success—that they are one mistake away from being found out. The truth? You're not an imposter. You're a leader in progress, just like everyone else. A little healthy fear keeps you humble and on your toes.

- **The "Role Model" Trap**

  Role models can be inspiring—but they can also be a trap if they pull us away from our authentic selves. Be honest: are you trying to become someone you admire, even if their style clashes with who you are? Maybe you admire a leader's command and influence but their aggressive approach leaves collateral damage. If that's not who you are, don't force it. True leadership isn't imitation. It's authenticity.

The best leaders create space for others to grow without asking them to change who they are. In my journey, I've been fortunate to work with leaders who supported my goals, celebrated my ambition, and respected me for being authentic—not for fitting into a mold. Great leadership isn't about forcing people to jump through hoops or prove their worth; it's about recognizing potential and encouraging people to lead from their true selves. You deserve that kind of leadership—and you have the power to offer it to others too.

Being You Is a Balancing Act: Tough vs. Compassionate

Early in my career, I got feedback that I needed to be "tougher" on my team. The perception was that I was too nice—not driving hard enough—and my boss even advised me to be "a bitch with a velvet glove."

At first, I struggled to find the right balance. I tried dialing up the toughness—even ruled with an iron fist a few times—but it didn't feel authentic. Doing so didn't get better results either. Both I and the people on the receiving end felt the tension. It wasn't the kind of leader I wanted to be.

I also didn't love hearing from team members later that they sometimes didn't like working for me. Their honesty stung. But it taught me something important: high standards alone aren't enough—how you lead people through those standards matters just as much. I needed to find a better way.

Over time, I learned that I could be demanding and compassionate. I focused first on building real relationships—understanding what mattered to each person—and then connected their personal goals to the broader team mission. That connection sparked intrinsic motivation—a fire to achieve that came from within, not from fear.

Years later, one of those same team members told me, "It was uncomfortable—your standards were so high—but looking back, it was one of the best experiences of my career. You cared. You challenged me. And you made me better."

That's the real journey of leadership: finding the balance between who you've been, who you are, and who you are becoming—where strength is rooted in care, challenge is delivered through connection, and growth is fueled by authenticity.

> "There is freedom waiting for you,
> On the breezes of the sky,
> And you ask 'What if I fall?'
> Oh but my darling,
> What if you fly?"
> —*Erin Hanson*

Progress over Perfection

As you work toward closing your gap, remind yourself: leadership growth is about progress, not perfection. There will be moments when you don't get it exactly right—when the balance between being tough and compassionate tips too far one way or the other. That's not failure; that's part of the journey. Real leadership isn't about flawless execution; it's about learning, adjusting, and continuing to move forward with intention.

One of the most powerful ways to stay on track is to journal your journey. Write down your goals, your small wins, the challenges you face, and how you respond. Tracking your progress helps you see how far you've come—and when you can look back, it's much easier to move forward with clarity and confidence. Leadership is built in the small, consistent steps you take each day. Keep showing up. Keep learning. Keep building the future you're meant for.

Find Your Supporters

If you want to become the best version of yourself, you can't do it alone—you need people who believe in you, push you, and lift you higher. Surround yourself with supporters who see your potential and fuel your ambition. True allies won't tear you down or compete with your dreams; they'll stand beside you and remind you who you're capable of becoming.

When I shared my bold vision of traveling the world, some people cheered and said, "That's amazing—how can I help?"

Others rolled their eyes and declared, "You'll never do that." Moments like that have taught me something critical: not everyone is meant to walk your path with you—and that's OK. The ones who matter will energize you, not drain you.

Find the people who raise your sights, spark your courage, and celebrate your growth. Build your inner circle wisely—because when you surround yourself with belief, levity, critical constructive feedback, positivity, and inspiration, you don't just dream bigger; you fly.

Bold Takeaways

- **Build a clear, focused plan and take the first step.** Big transformations don't happen overnight. Set clear goals, start small, and build momentum with consistent, focused action.

- **Prioritize progress over perfection.** Growth isn't about getting everything right the first time; it's about learning, adjusting, and moving forward with courage. Track your progress, celebrate your small wins, and keep showing up for your future self.

- **Lead with authenticity while raising your standards.** Real leadership is balancing strength with care, challenge with connection. You don't have to change who you are—you have to lean fully into who you're becoming.

- **Surround yourself with believers and builders.** Your circle matters. Find people who fuel your ambition, spark your courage, and lift you higher—because with the right support, you don't just move forward; you soar.

Chapter 6:
Leadership Development Plan Exercise

Use the following template to create your leadership development plan.

BOLD Leadership Development Plan Template

1. Personal Leadership Vision and Gaps
- Statement:

What kind of leader do you aspire to be? What impact do you want to have on your team, organization, or community? If you were really being BOLD, what would you achieve? Where are the gaps from where you are and where you want to be?

Example: "I aspire to be an empathetic and strategic leader who fosters innovation, empowers my team, and drives meaningful impact."

2. Leadership Goals
- Goal 1:

Example: Improve emotional intelligence by enhancing self-awareness and empathy.

- Goal 2:

Example: Strengthen strategic thinking to align team goals with organizational priorities.

- Goal 3:

Example: Enhance public-speaking skills to improve executive presence.

3. Strengths and Development Areas
- Strengths to Leverage:

Example: Strong problem-solving skills, ability to build trust, excellent work ethic

- Areas for Development:

Example: Delegation, active listening, effective conflict management

4. Action Steps for Each Goal

Goal 1: Improve Emotional Intelligence

- Action 1: Enroll in an emotional-intelligence workshop.
- Action 2: Dedicate 15 minutes weekly to journaling reflections on interactions.
- Action 3: Seek regular feedback from peers and team members on communication and listening skills.

Goal 2: Strengthen Strategic Thinking

- Action 1: Read one strategy-focused book or complete an online course within the next three months.
- Action 2: Apply new strategic frameworks to a current team project.
- Action 3: Schedule monthly one-on-one meetings with a mentor to discuss strategic decision-making.

Goal 3: Enhance Public-Speaking Skills

- Action 1: Join a public-speaking group, such as Toastmasters.
- Action 2: Record and review practice presentations to refine delivery and tone.
- Action 3: Deliver three presentations to leadership within the next six months and gather feedback.

5. Resources Needed

- Books/Courses:

Example: Emotional Intelligence 2.0, Harvard Business Review articles, online leadership courses

- Mentors or Coaches:

Example: Executive coach for public speaking, peer mentor for feedback

- Tools or Technology:

Example: Feedback tools (e.g., 360 evaluations), project-management software for goal tracking

6. Metrics for Success
- Goal 1:

Example: Achieve a 20-percent improvement in emotional-intelligence ratings from a 360 feedback survey within six months.
- Goal 2:

Example: Successfully implement a new strategic initiative and achieve project objectives within 90 days.
- Goal 3:

Example: Receive a 90-percent positive rating on public-speaking clarity and impact from leadership peers by the end of the quarter.

7. Timeline
- Immediate (Next 30 Days):

Example: Enroll in workshops and identify mentors.
- Short Term (3–6 Months):

Example: Complete training programs, execute smaller actionable steps, and track early progress.
- Long Term (6–12 Months):

Example: Measure success against KPIs, refine skills, and evaluate results to plan next steps.

8. Accountability and Check-Ins
- Plan for Check-Ins:

Example: Schedule monthly self-assessments and quarterly meetings with a mentor or coach to review progress.
- Feedback Mechanisms:

Example: Use surveys, peer feedback, or performance reviews to track improvement.

9. Reflection and Adjustments
- Reflection Questions:
  - What progress have I made toward my goals?
  - What challenges am I facing, and how can I address them?
  - What adjustments do I need to make to stay aligned with my vision?
- Next Steps:

Update the plan as needed to reflect growth and new aspirations.

Chapter 7

How BOLD Leaders Rise Above Weakness

"Success isn't about fixing what's broken—it's about doubling down on what makes you unstoppable."
—Kim Svoboda

The simple fact is that the highest performers in the world invest in and leverage their strengths. It seems obvious, yet most of us do the opposite. We work harder at the things we aren't good at and, in the pursuit of trying to be good at everything, become mediocre at most.

The secret ingredient to creating a high-performance culture comes from leveraging what people do well versus trying to change them into something they're not or make them good at everything.

Hello, leaders, did you catch that?

Stop trying to make yourself and your team into perfect little clones that are good at everything you're good at and even look just like you. Instead, empower them to utilize their strengths. Whatever time you spend working on trying to change them into someone they are not is a colossal waste. We share more on this later in the book, but suffice it to say, let them do it their way and watch them flourish. Real ROI comes from investing in the areas where you have talent. Taking that talent and turning it into a strength, where you have near-perfect performance every time, is where BOLD thrives!

Knowing My Strengths

I was on an impossible journey early in my leadership career to be great at everything. I found myself banging my head against the wall repeatedly. The harder I worked at being "great at everything" and focused strictly on developing my weaknesses, the more discouraged I became. In fact, I might not have been open to the message of playing to my strengths except I was at one of my lowest points in my career and knew something needed to change.

I happened upon a discussion between Oprah Winfrey and Marcus Buckingham and got very curious. Buckingham, a well-known strengths-based performance advocate, emphasized the importance of focusing on what you are naturally good at rather than trying to fix your weaknesses. He advocated for identifying your unique strengths and then consistently using them as the foundation for your personal and professional growth.

One of his key messages was that individuals should know their strengths and actively find ways to use them more often in their daily activities. By doing so, people can be more engaged, more productive, and ultimately more successful.

Expert tip: Play to your strengths—invest in them and use them as often as possible. Don't try to make weaknesses into strengths; it's not going to happen. Manage around your weaknesses.

This completely changed my view on my personal development, as well as the way that I was approaching my team.

How Did I Get Here?

Well, I was considering taking on a new role at the request of a leader who wanted me to start up a new function in the company. I was concerned because this new department was not really in my wheelhouse; it would be extremely operational, finance, project management, and detail oriented—and that isn't where my strengths were. When I expressed doubts, my boss assured me that it would be fine, that I'd do a great job, and that this role was greatly needed. So I said yes.

It became clear very quickly that this would be one of the hardest jobs I had ever had. Reporting, analysis, financial details, consolidating commission plans, space planning, endless projects, and many people bearing "gifts" of tasks they didn't want to do anymore because they were "operational." The job required high attention to detail and excellent project-management skills. If you look at my strengths profile, there's nothing in it that says I excel with details or even execution. Can I get things done? Of course I can, but it's not where my talents lie or what I enjoy doing most.

So here I was in a job I hated, being too much of a pleaser and overpromising and suffering greatly. I dreaded going to work and was miserable. The company went through some big changes at the same time, and ultimately, my boss began to hate his job too, which didn't help matters one bit. But I digress—back to strengths.

After hearing Marcus and Oprah's conversation, I thought to myself: *Well, I am definitely not playing to my strengths right now and I am MISERABLE. What if I tried this? What if I figured out what it is that I like to do and then try to do more of it? What do I have to lose?* The answer to that last question was "nothing," so off I went on this new journey to pursue my talents and turn them into strengths.

I bought the *StrengthsFinder 2.0* book and took the assessment. When I looked at my results, my eyes were opened to the things that deep down I mostly knew but was overlooking. My strengths included "big-picture," "people-oriented" talents such as strategic thinking, influencing others, and relationship building. No top strengths in execution and details, which were what my current role was over-indexed on. At least, this was the way I was approaching it. According to my CliftonStrengths profile, I was approaching my work all wrong. It was no wonder I felt absolutely paralyzed.

That's when clarity struck me: *I need to leverage my strengths and be more strategic in my approach. Instead of trying to do everything, I must insist on getting the right people on my team to get the work done.*

After that key moment, things started to turn around. I could feel the change. As I was more intentional about playing to my strengths and not trying to focus on the things I stunk at, my performance got better. My whole LIFE got better.

This strengths-based approach positively impacted me so much that I decided to share it with my team. I could almost hear the light-bulbs turn on, watching my team members identify and unleash their talents on their work and our team. This powerful secret decoder ring enriched our team's performance, and we experienced dramatic improvement.

Identifying Your Strengths

I loved my business and psychology classes in college. In fact, I could have earned a minor in psychology with just two more classes—but I decided against it. One was abnormal psychology, which I watched many classmates struggle through, and the other was statistics (that elusive analytical talent showing up early!). Even back then, I naturally gravitated toward the people side of business: what makes individuals thrive and how that connects to success.

Don Clifton, known as the father of strengths-based psychology and the creator of CliftonStrengths, had the same instinct. Rather than focusing on what's wrong with people, he spent decades studying what leads to excellence.[vii] Through years of research, Clifton and his team identified over 400 attributes that contribute to human success and distilled them into 34 core talent themes.[viii] These 34 themes give individuals a language to understand their natural talents and a clear path to develop them into real strengths intentionally.[ix]

Today, I use CliftonStrengths in nearly all my coaching and leadership programs because a strengths-based approach helps people discover where they can contribute most, where they'll find the most energy and engagement, and where they'll truly stand out. Knowing and investing in your strengths isn't just personal development; it's a strategy for building a fulfilling and successful life.

Leveraging Your Strengths

Identifying your talents is just the first step. Reflect on how these talents have contributed to your past achievements. Often, you might not even recognize that you're using a specific strength during critical moments. For instance, if empathy is one of your core strengths, think back to a time when you supported your team through a challenging period—your empathetic nature was likely a key factor in helping them persevere. If we ignore the emotions our teams are feeling, especially in times of stress, they may feel that we don't truly understand. Acknowledging the distress and allowing team members to express their emotions can enable them to feel heard and better able to move forward with the solution.

If at first you don't succeed, try again.

Consider my strength: strategic thinking. It proved essential when my team was stuck in a project. By deploying this talent, I could see the end of the project, where we would achieve success. It wasn't an easy path to take, but we worked together to devise multiple strategies and tried them. My strategic-thinking talent automatically came up with contingency plans. Plan A didn't work. Plan B seemed promising but also didn't pan out. Eventually, a modified version of Plan C brought us success.

Now back to your talents; let's turn your focus to the present. *How are your strengths manifesting in your daily activities? Are they propelling you toward success, or do they sometimes create blind spots?* Reflecting on this can reveal how you might use your strengths more intentionally or develop them further. A start-stop-continue exercise can help you decide what to do and what not to do in order to leverage this talent.

Enhancing Your Talents to Turn Them into Strengths

Think about how you can enhance your strengths. For example, if you excel in analytics, consider taking a specialized course to deepen your understanding and apply your analytical skills more effectively in your business. Or could you sign up for a project where such skills would be leveraged and enhanced? Investing in your strengths boosts your proficiency and enhances your overall performance. It also feels good because you are doing what comes naturally and your growth happens quickly.

Take my approach with communication: despite it being my top talent, I have worked with several coaches, for business and for communication. Though it might seem unusual to seek coaching in an area where you're already proficient, doing so can lead to remarkable growth. My goal of being recognized as a top speaker in a professional group I frequently address has motivated me to further refine this skill with my communication coach. By improving in this area, I will also become better as a leader, and an executive coach, so it's a big win. I want to emphasize an important shift in perspective—instead of seeking help only in areas where we lack talent, let's focus on enhancing our existing strengths. By doing so, we can experience exponential growth in our capabilities and performance. Investing in your talents makes development more enjoyable and impactful, allowing for incredible growth in areas that come naturally to you. Investing in talents to turn them into strengths while achieving work goals involves strategic planning and intentional actions.

Here are some steps you can follow to maximize your potential and achieve objectives effectively:

- **Identify core talents.** Begin by thoroughly assessing your innate talents, possibly using tools such as the CliftonStrengths assessment or similar methodologies. Understand which natural abilities contribute most to your success.
- **Set specific goals.** Align your talents with your professional goals. Set SMART objectives that leverage your strengths to enhance productivity and efficiency at work.
- **Seek feedback and mentorship.** Regular feedback from peers, subordinates, and superiors can lend insight into how your talents are impacting your work and where you can improve.

Additionally, finding a mentor who excels in areas related to your talents can provide guidance and accelerate your development.

- **Engage in targeted training.** Invest in specialized training programs that strengthen your talents. Whether it's leadership training, technical-skills development, or strategic-thinking workshops, targeted learning can transform a raw talent into a formidable strength. Hire a coach to help you invest in your talent in order to strengthen it.

- **Apply talents in new projects.** Actively seek or create opportunities to apply your strengths in new and challenging projects. This reinforces your abilities and showcases to others in the organization your competence and versatility.

- **Hire and delegate to cover weaknesses.** Understand that not all areas are or need to be your strengths. Delegate tasks outside your strengths to trusted team members who excel in those disciplines. Doing so will improve overall team performance and allow you to focus on the areas where you can make the most impact.

- **Practice reflective leadership.** Regularly reflect on your progress and reassess your goals. Reflective practice can help you both understand how effectively you use your strengths and adjust your strategies.

- **Cultivate a strengths-based culture.** Encourage your team to identify and use their strengths. This boosts team morale and productivity and creates a supportive environment where everyone can thrive. (More on this later.)

- **Measure and adjust.** Continuously measure the outcomes of your efforts against your set goals. Use these insights to refine your approach and align your strengths with your objectives better.

- **Celebrate successes and learn from setbacks.** Recognize and celebrate when you achieve milestones using your strengths. Equally important is learning from setbacks in order to understand what adjustments must be made.

By following these steps, you can effectively turn your natural talents into robust strengths, creating a powerful foundation for achieving personal and professional success and fostering a positive work environment.

What If Your Strength Is Getting in the Way?

Sometimes your strength might also be the thing that's getting in your way because you're overusing it or not using it in the most productive way. One of our partners, E2grow, came up with a great list of each type of talent and how it looks when you are using it maturely versus when it is raw. It's a great resource that we use with our clients.

Let's take the example of one leader we worked with who had recently been promoted. John was well known within his organization as the go-to person for getting things done. With an innate talent for execution, he would work tirelessly, often taking on most action items himself to ensure that every task was completed to the highest standard. His dedication and ability to deliver results consistently were eventually recognized with a well-deserved promotion. However, the new role marked a significant shift from his previous position. Instead of primarily focusing on execution, John was now required to adopt a more strategic approach, lead with vision, and empower his team members to take on more responsibilities to bring the vision to reality.

Initially, John found the transition challenging. Accustomed to a hands-on approach, he struggled to adapt to his new role's broader, more abstract responsibilities. This led to him falling behind and inadvertently causing frustration among his team members, who felt over-managed and stifled. Recognizing these issues, we worked closely with John to shift his focus. By scheduling dedicated time for strategic thinking and planning, he began to see the bigger picture beyond immediate tasks. We coached him on leadership techniques that emphasized empowerment and trust, encouraging him to support his team's autonomy through regular but nonintrusive check-ins. These adjustments helped John evolve into a leader who sets the vision and inspires his team to achieve it independently.

"My Money Is on You"

Within the first few weeks of joining a new organization, I was asked to present my regional quarterly business review. The audience consisted of the C-suite and my peers in marketing and sales. During my presentation, I shared my observations so far and where we'd be investing our time and effort. There was a consultant in the room that the company had hired to help with sales strategy. He came up to introduce himself and leaned in and said to me, privately, "My money's on you."

Surprised, I looked at him, "What do you mean your money's on me? What are you betting?"

"You're going to be the top-performing sales leader in the next 12 months," he affirmed.

Flattered, I replied, "Wow. Thank you for the vote of confidence, but why would you say so?"

"You're focused on something the other leaders are not: the culture of your team. With that, your experience, and your leadership, my money is on you."

As I worked with my new team to chart our BOLD path, we made a deliberate decision: simplify, focus, and lead with our strengths. We stripped away the noise and zeroed in on doing a few critical things exceptionally well. At the same time, we helped each person identify and lean into their unique strengths. Once we aligned around this approach, performance soared. Every key metric improved dramatically—and before long, we were leading the way.

Taking the BOLD path isn't easy. When a senior leader pulled me aside to point out that I was doing things differently, he definitely wasn't complimentary about it. In that moment, it would have been easy to second-guess myself. Others in the organization openly questioned my approach—at times, some even told me outright that they thought I was barking up the wrong tree.

When everyone else is following the crowd, the pressure to blend in can be overwhelming. But true leadership isn't about conformity—it's about standing your ground, leading with integrity, and holding fast to your vision, even when the road feels lonely.

In the end, staying the course made all the difference. The moment I saw more members of our team than ever before crossing the stage at our national sales conference, recognized for their record-breaking success, I knew we were on the right path.

BOLD Takeaways

- **Stop trying to fix everything—focus on where you're strong.** Success doesn't come from fixing weaknesses; it comes from doubling down on what makes you unstoppable. High performers invest in their strengths and manage around their gaps.

- **Know your strengths—and own them.** Getting crystal clear on your talents is the first step. Your greatest breakthroughs happen when you build your life and leadership around what you naturally do best. Move them from raw to mature.

- **Grow what comes naturally—and grow fast.** When you invest in developing your natural strengths, you grow faster, enjoy your work more, and create bigger impact. Growth is exponential when it's built on a foundation of talent.

- **Stand your ground—even when others doubt you.** Taking the BOLD path means trusting your strengths and your vision, even when the pressure to conform is high. True leaders stay the course and create extraordinary results.

Chapter 7:
BOLD Leadership Development Plan
Strengths-Refinement Exercise

Go back to your BOLD Leadership Development Plan that you completed in chapter 6 and refine it with your newfound learning on strengths, focusing on section 3:

Strengths and Development Areas

- Strengths to Leverage:

Example: Strong problem-solving skills, ability to build trust, excellent work ethic

- Areas for Development:

Example: Delegation, active listening, managing conflict effectively

Chapter 8

BOLD Leaders Stay Strong When Others Break

"I can be changed by what happens to me. But I refuse to be reduced by it. Each challenge is an opportunity to grow stronger and more capable."
—Maya Angelou

Resilience isn't about bouncing back; it's about coming back stronger. Resilience is increasingly recognized as a critical attribute for effective leadership, especially in today's fast-paced and often unpredictable business environment. The research on resilience in leadership focuses on how leaders can withstand stress, adapt to change, and recover quickly from challenges.[x]

Throughout my career, many leaders I worked with treated their bodies and minds like crap. Surviving rather than thriving. This resistance to change can prevent leaders from exploring innovative solutions that enhance their resilience and effectiveness. It can also be sneaky, this impact on resilience. Maybe you didn't realize that your workouts had dwindled and you weren't sleeping as well as in the past, and the number of late-night cheeseburgers was steadily climbing as you prioritized everything other than yourself. Sometimes leaders don't wake up until they have had a major career hiccup or health scare, and that might be too late. BOLD leaders work on their resilience to make sure that doesn't happen. Nobody's perfect, so when BOLD leaders get off track, they recognize it and course correct.

It's worth working through resilience-building challenges in order to be the best leader possible. We've found that resilience is a cornerstone of effective leadership, enabling leaders to guide their teams through challenges with strength and adaptability. For leaders, maintaining a regimen of healthy eating, ample sleep, and regular exercise is not just about personal health but also about setting a standard of care that reflects their commitment to their role.

What Gets in the Way?

Taking time to listen to yourself is a big part of renewal and self-care. Yet we don't listen to ourselves nearly as much as we should. How could we? We have noise going on around us all the time! But what if, instead of surrounding ourselves with all that noise, we gave ourselves time to be quiet, to take a walk in the woods, to do more meditation, or do the thing that helps us find inner harmony?

So what gets in the way?

Here are a few issues:

- **Time Constraints.** Many leaders are under constant pressure to meet immediate deadlines while managing day-to-day operations. This relentless pace can make prioritizing long-term resilience strategies such as training, personal development, or wellness programs difficult.
- **Stigma Around Vulnerability.** In many corporate cultures, there remains a stigma associated with showing vulnerability. Leaders may fear that admitting the need for resilience strategies, such as stress management or mental-health support, could be seen as a sign of weakness. This perception can discourage leaders from seeking help in order to build resilience. I once worked for a leader who told us it was OK to request a mental-health day if we needed one, but we all knew that wasn't actually the case and that he would keep score and ultimately hold it against us.

- **Lack of Awareness or Understanding.** Some leaders may not fully understand what resilience entails or its importance. Without a clear recognition of the benefits that resilience can bring, such as improved decision-making under pressure and better team morale, leaders might not invest in developing this crucial skill set.
- **Perceived Cost.** Investing in resilience, whether through programs, workshops, or personal coaching, often requires upfront financial and time commitments. Leaders might struggle to justify these investments if the immediate benefits are not clearly measurable—as there are only so many hours in a day—or when budgets are tight.
- **Difficulty in Measuring Impact.** Resilience benefits might not be as immediately apparent or straightforward to quantify as other business metrics. This difficulty in measurement can be an obstacle for leaders trying to demonstrate to stakeholders the value of resilience-building activities or to justify ongoing investment in these areas.

Building Resilience

If you are not actively building resilience, you're passively eroding it. What can you do about that?

If you want to lead at your highest level, building resilience is non-negotiable. BOLD leaders don't just survive the hard seasons—they thrive through them. And it's not by accident. They deliberately create habits that protect their energy, sharpen their minds, and strengthen their hearts.

When you take care of yourself, you're not being selfish—you're being strategic. You're honoring your role, your potential, and your team. Because without resilience, even the most talented leaders eventually burn out or break down.

1. Prioritize Physical Health

Great leadership starts with great energy—and great energy comes from taking care of your physical health. This isn't just about personal wellness; it's about leadership effectiveness. Leaders who fuel their bodies well, are consistently on the move, and get plenty of deep, restful sleep make better decisions, stay more composed under pressure, and lead their teams through challenges with strength and clarity.

Here's what BOLD leaders know:

- **Eat to fuel performance.** Proper nutrition isn't about diets or deprivation; it's about nourishing your brain and body with the fuel they need to operate at a high level: eating nutrient-dense foods, staying hydrated, and being mindful of habits that sabotage your performance, such as excessive alcohol consumption. What you put in your body directly impacts your clarity of thought, your resilience under stress, and your stamina through long days and hard seasons. Fuel yourself like the leader you are becoming—your future self deserves it.

- **Move your body every day. Regular exercise is a must if you want to lead at your best.** Physical activity reduces symptoms of depression and anxiety, boosts your mood, sharpens your focus, and increases your resilience against the daily stresses of leadership. You don't have to train for a marathon, as even consistent walks, strength training, or yoga can create powerful shifts in your energy and outlook.

- **Protect your sleep like your future depends on it—because it does.** Sleep is the ultimate performance enhancer. It directly impacts cognitive functions such as memory, decision-making, creativity, and emotional regulation. Leaders who consistently prioritize quality sleep are calmer under pressure, better problem-solvers, and stronger communicators. When you're sleep deprived, your leadership takes a hit—and so does your team.

Here's the truth: If you are consistently running on junk food, stress, and only four hours of sleep, you are not leading at your highest potential—no matter how hard you work. Your body and mind are your greatest leadership assets. Protect them fiercely.

Think of every meal, every workout, and every night of sleep as a direct investment in your leadership performance.

Leaders often say, "I'm just working particularly hard right now. I'll take care of myself later."

But "later" rarely comes—and when it does, the cost of waiting is often much higher than you'd expect.

Research backs this up. Studies, including one from Stanford University, have found that once you go beyond 50 hours a week, your productivity per hour sharply declines. More than 55 hours and there's zero productivity gain—and your health, creativity, and resilience start paying the price.

BOLD leaders don't wait for burnout to force them to change.

They invest in their resilience daily—because they know that their teams, their missions, and their futures depend on it.

2. Build Mental Toughness

The best leaders aren't just smart—they're mentally tough. They have the grit, focus, and emotional endurance to navigate uncertainty, setbacks, and pressure without crumbling. Mental toughness isn't something you're born with; it's something you build through intentional practice.

Here's how BOLD leaders strengthen their mental resilience:

- **Develop mindfulness and emotional regulation.** Mindfulness isn't just a buzzword; it's a leadership superpower. Leaders who practice mindfulness are better able to stay calm under pressure, separate fact from emotion, and respond thoughtfully rather than react impulsively. Simple practices such as five minutes of intentional breathing, gratitude journaling, or guided meditation can dramatically improve your emotional control and decision-making during high-stakes situations.

- **Embrace adversity as training.** Mentally tough leaders don't see obstacles as signs to stop—they see them as invitations to grow stronger. Each challenge, each "failure," and each hard day is part of the training ground that sharpens resilience. When things get tough, ask yourself, *"What is this challenge trying to teach me?"* That simple mindset shift turns setbacks into stepping stones for greater strength.

- **Control what you can; release what you can't.** Trying to control everything is a fast track to burnout and frustration. Mentally tough leaders know the difference between what's in their control (effort, attitude, preparation) and what's not (other people's opinions, external events). They stay grounded by focusing on their "circle of control," freeing up energy for meaningful action instead of wasting it on things they can't change.

A simple but powerful mantra to remember comes from Mel Robbins's book *The Let Them Theory*. "Let them judge. Let them misunderstand. Let them doubt. That's not your work. Your work is to stay true to your vision, your values, and your growth."[xi]

When you let go of needing others' approval or trying to change their minds, you liberate yourself to move faster, think clearer, and lead stronger. Focus on what you can control. Let the rest go. That's how resilient, BOLD leaders rise above the noise and keep building the future they believe in.

Expert tip: Build your "mental fitness" daily. Just like you wouldn't expect your body to get stronger without regular training, you can't expect mental toughness to just "show up" when you need it. Build it daily: Practice mindfulness. Face small discomforts (take the cold shower, have the hard conversation). Stretch your comfort zone deliberately. Celebrate every time you persevere when it would be easier to quit.

Mental toughness does not mean you are fearless. It means you face fear, stress, and pressure—and move forward anyway.

Leaders who master mental toughness:
- make better decisions under stress,
- navigate change with greater agility, and
- inspire confidence and stability in their teams—even when storms are raging around them.

Here's the secret. When you invest daily in your mental fitness—just like you do with your physical fitness—resilience becomes your default setting, not something you have to scramble to find when everything goes sideways.

3. Reframe Challenges as Growth Opportunities

Mentally tough leaders don't crumble under pressure—they convert that pressure into power. They view setbacks, challenges, and even failures not as evidence that they're "not good enough" but rather as essential training grounds for growth.

Instead of asking, "Why is this happening to me?" they ask, "What is this here to teach me?"

When something hard shows up—a tough client, a missed goal, a team setback—it's easy to zero in on the obstacle and lose perspective.

One of my favorite exercises is to literally stand up, turn my body around, and face away from whatever problem I'm stuck on. It's not just about moving physically—I'm also reminding myself to mentally shift my focus. By turning my back on the problem, I remind myself that while challenges are behind me, new ideas and opportunities are in front of me if I choose to see them. It's a simple way to remember that where you look—both in your mind and with your body—is where you'll move next. Reframing like this isn't just wishful thinking; it's a strategy for staying resilient and moving forward. Reframing isn't just about positive thinking; it's also about strategic resilience.

Every elite performer, from world-class athletes to visionary CEOs, builds mental toughness not by avoiding hardship but by interpreting it differently. When something hard shows up, self-doubt is an easy trap. Resist it. Step back and reframe the challenge by asking yourself:

- "What skill can I strengthen here?"
- "How will overcoming this make me better, wiser, and stronger for what's ahead?"
- "Where's the hidden gift in this obstacle?"

Reframing isn't just positive thinking—it's strategic thinking.

ACTION:

The next time adversity shows up, don't react. Instead, take a pause and write down three ways this challenge could make you better. You'll be shocked at how much power this simple shift gives you.

4. Strengthen Your Inner Voice

Your internal dialogue is either your secret weapon or your silent enemy. Mentally tough leaders cultivate an inner voice that is encouraging, realistic, and focused on resilience. They don't let their inner critic run wild. They train their mind to coach themselves forward, especially when the pressure is on.

Instead of beating themselves up with such thoughts as:
- "I'm not cut out for this,"
- "I always mess up," or
- "I'll never figure this out,"

mentally tough leaders tell themselves:
- "I'm learning. I'm growing. I'm making progress,"
- "This challenge is tough—and so am I," or
- "I have what it takes. Let's figure it out."

It's not about lying to yourself. It's about leading yourself—through setbacks, uncertainty, and risk.

Journal Prompt: Create a personal mantra—a short phrase that reminds you of your strength when you need it most. Write it down. Post it somewhere visible. Say it whenever the going gets tough. Train your inner coach to be louder than your inner critic.

Be Intentional and Take a Break

Many leaders maintain the notion that "there's no good time to take a vacation." I strongly disagree. Prioritizing time off for renewal is essential. Without proper self-care, you cannot perform your best work. It's crucial to take those vacation days.

For many, renewal comes in the form of a vacation. In my case, it could mean spending quality time with my family or going to Mexico with my girlfriends every year, reliving our college days, hanging out on the beach with our endless discussions about everything. These experiences are rejuvenating. I return feeling fantastic, having reconnected with my friends and, in a way, with my youthful, fun-loving self.

Renewal might also mean stepping out of your comfort zone to accomplish something new, such as hiking across difficult terrain, completing a triathlon, or taking up a new hobby or challenge that surprises those around you.

You must plan for renewal; it doesn't just happen on its own.

Every summer, I carve out intentional time for renewal. I head to my local botanical garden when the weather is perfect, leave my laptop at home, silence my phone, and bring only my journal. Surrounded by nature's beauty, I give myself the space to think, dream, and reconnect. It's not just relaxing; it's catalytic. I always walk away energized, focused, and ready to move forward.

What About You?

What does true renewal look like in your life? Maybe it's a months-long sabbatical, a three-day getaway, or even a simple 48-hour retreat into the woods like some leaders I know do every year.

But renewal doesn't have to be big in order to be powerful. Maybe for you it's just one hour—a walk without your phone, a quiet cup of coffee alone, a visit to a place that inspires you.

The key is intentionality. Pause long enough to define what renewal looks like for you, then schedule it.

If you don't make space for renewal, the demands of life and leadership will consume every available inch.

I learned this firsthand at a leadership retreat that transformed how I lead. Before we left, we completed 360 feedback surveys, gaining raw insights from our teams and peers. Then during the retreat, we dug deep, reconnecting to the organization's values, uncovering what truly motivated us, and tackling business simulations that forced us to lead in real time under pressure.

Stepping away from the daily grind gave us a new perspective—on ourselves, on each other, and on our shared future. We returned not just recharged but recalibrated—better leaders and a stronger team.

The truth is that you rarely realize how heavy the weight of your daily grind has become until you step away from it. Whether it's a retreat, a vacation, or even a bold life decision such as leaving a draining job, doubling down on your own renewal is never wasted.

It's an investment—in your clarity, your leadership, and your future resilience.

Building resilience isn't a luxury for leaders; it's a necessity. The future demands leaders who don't just survive tough times but rise stronger because of them. Maintaining your physical health, developing mental toughness, reframing setbacks as growth opportunities, and strengthening your inner voice are the four pillars that create a resilient, BOLD leader. Resilience isn't built when things are easy; it's forged when you choose to protect your energy, sharpen your mind, and fuel your strength even when it's difficult. Self-care isn't selfish; it's a strategic investment in your leadership future. Renewal isn't accidental; it's intentional. Every habit you build now is a down payment on your ability to thrive later. BOLD leaders don't wait for crisis to build resilience. They build it daily so when the storm comes—and it always does—they're ready to lead through it with power, clarity, and heart.

BOLD Takeaways

- **Protect your physical energy like it's your greatest asset.** High performance starts with high energy. Prioritize eating well, moving daily, getting good sleep, and treating your body like the leadership machine it is.

- **Build mental toughness through daily discipline.** Strengthen your mind the same way you strengthen your body—with daily practices that challenge your focus, emotional control, and resilience.

- **Reframe challenges as your leadership training ground.** When adversity hits, don't crumble; instead, pivot. Look away from the obstacle and toward the opportunities. Every setback holds the seeds of your next level of strength.

- **Train your inner voice to coach you forward.** Your internal dialogue is either your greatest weapon or your biggest weakness. Choose words that strengthen, encourage, and propel you forward—especially whenever the pressure is highest.

Chapter 8:
Stay Strong Playbook Exercise

Instructions

This isn't just about bouncing back; it's about bouncing forward. Use this playbook to *reset your resilience*, strengthen your leadership under pressure, and show up as your boldest self. Move through each step intentionally. Reflect. Commit. Take action. Revisit as needed. This is your personal resilience lab.

1. Get Real About Where You Are
Objective: Own your starting line.
Moves: Reflect honestly. How are you handling pressure?
Spot your stress triggers and default reactions—no judgment, just awareness.

2. Define Your Resilience Target
Objective: Set a bold goal for the leader you're becoming.
Moves: Pick one or two resilience muscles to build—such as emotional control or stress recovery.
Make it crystal clear and measurable (e.g., daily 10-minute mindfulness wins).

3. Build Your Power Skills
Objective: Strengthen what makes you unstoppable.
Moves: Sharpen your adaptability, emotional regulation, and communication edge.
Level up daily—through podcasts, coaches, books, or real-world reps.

4. Fortify Your Inner Circle
Objective: Surround yourself with strength, not noise.
Moves: Identify the people who lift you higher (and weed out the drainers).
Lean in—ask for support, share real conversations, and build trust.

5. Protect Your Energy Like a Pro

Objective: Fuel the machine—your body powers your mind.

Moves: Prioritize sleep, eating well, and daily movement.

Think like an elite athlete—recovery is not a luxury; it's your secret weapon.

6. Reflect, Reframe, Refuel

Objective: Turn every setback into a springboard.

Moves: Journal weekly. What worked? What didn't? What's next?

Reframe challenges as training—your resilience is always under construction.

7. Schedule Nonnegotiable Renewal

Objective: Recharge before you flatline.

Moves: Build breaks into your week and commit to them, like appointments you can't cancel.

Use nature, movement, laughter, creativity—whatever restores your fire.

8. Review, Celebrate, and Raise the Bar

Objective: Keep growing, never coasting.

Moves: Review your resilience plan every quarter.

Celebrate what's stronger—and set a new stretch target.

Lighthouse Leadership

Strong Vision, Stronger Teams

"BOLD leaders are lighthouses—unwavering in storms, silent in strength, and a safe guide home."
—Kim Svoboda

CDW, the powerhouse tech company where I was fortunate enough to start my professional career, was a place unlike any other—a company built on an unshakable culture of customer obsession, hard work, and shared success. What began in 1984 with Michael Krasny selling a single computer grew into a multibillion-dollar technology leader recognized on the Fortune 500. Along the way, CDW became known not just for explosive growth but for a culture where coworkers were celebrated, customers came first, and results consistently exceeded expectations. That kind of sustained success didn't happen by chance. It started with the leader. Michael set the tone, and the culture followed.

Michael Krasny was our lighthouse. To know what to do, we only had to look at him—passionately focused on customers, generously rewarding coworkers, and never afraid of rolling up his sleeves. He often reminded us that "success means never being satisfied," urging constant improvement. He reinforced that "it's only good if it's win/win," making clear that real success creates value for everyone. And he believed that "good luck many times comes disguised as hard work," showing us that leadership meant modeling effort, not expecting others to carry the load alone.

BOLD leaders embody the essence of lighthouse leadership, illuminating the path forward for our organizations and teams, just as the lighthouse does for mariners. They constantly shine a light for others to find their way. Without this perspective, our teams would be fumbling around in the dark, getting nowhere.

BOLD leaders understand that it is our responsibility to cast light on the journey ahead. We remember that we are the ones with the courage to go first in order to light the path for others to join us.

Building a Strong Bench

Once, a client brought me in because their CEO, Christine, had a pressing concern: client relationships were suffering. Despite their team being proficient in task execution, they lacked the necessary acumen for building and nurturing connections. They would finish their work and have nothing else lined up to work on next because they weren't communicating effectively with their clients. A CliftonStrengths assessment unveiled this critical gap.

When I presented Christine with the team grid, she seemed content, which caught me off guard. The team was very strong in the domain of execution but was missing the other critical domains of strategic thinking, influencing, and—surprise, surprise—relationship building. When I hinted at exploring other essential domains that would be critical in communicating with their clients, such as influencing, strategic thinking, and relationship building, she simply brushed it off.

They had been outsourcing certain functions that were helping to cover some of their gaps, and she leaned in a lot to cover those gaps, but she was only one person, and the firm was growing rapidly. Christine brought me in to help them build better relationships with their clients. In addition to my work with their team, I proposed recruiting individuals who could complement the team's strengths, bringing in experts to cover their gaps. I emphasized the value of diverse skill sets in enhancing team dynamics. Yet Christine remained unconvinced—until I appealed to her bottom line.

Highlighting the cost-effectiveness of hiring individuals with these strengths over stretching herself too thin and filling gaps with outsourcing, I helped her realize the long-term benefits of diversifying the profile of her team. Investing in team members with better relationship-building capabilities promised greater efficiency and effectiveness, ultimately positively impacting the bottom line. In addition to saving them money, employees working for the organization and having buy-in to the overall goals and relationship building would approach their work with a passion and depth that a consultant couldn't come close to.

Understanding the potential return on investment, Christine reconsidered, recognizing the value of a well-rounded team. In the end, prioritizing diverse strengths and capabilities would not only enhance client relations but also bolster the company's overall success. They built this into their hiring plan, and I'm happy to report that they have grown significantly and are enjoying great success.

Qualities of a Lighthouse Leader

Before we get into the *how* of lighthouse leadership, let's consider the qualities needed to be a lighthouse leader.

To be a lighthouse leader, you'll need to do the following:

- **Have the ability to empower others.** Your job is to help your people discover their strengths, and you can only do that by empowering them to use their skills, not your own (we'll get into that soon), in their job.
- **Be effective at communication.** Listen far more than you speak, and actively consider the concerns, ideas, and feedback of the team. You will demonstrate that you care about their well-being and are committed to their success. Then, clearly share the vision and goals and ensure that everyone understands what we are doing and why it matters.
- **Be a good coach.** You want to be someone who will guide your team, help them course-correct as needed, reinforce the good, and feel connected to the vision and team.
- **Treat others with respect**. Not only is it the right thing to do, but it is also the foundation of trust and collaboration within the team.
- **Take responsibility.** Own up to your mistakes (and those of your team), learn from them, and take steps to fix any issues. By

taking ownership of it all, you show your team what it means to have accountability.

With these qualities, you will not only encourage your team but also create a culture of empowerment and trust. When team members begin to leverage their strengths and work effectively toward an organization's shared objectives and goals, the true magic transpires.

Through lighthouse leadership, we guide the way, inspiring and empowering those around us to navigate the challenges ahead and achieve success.

How? Let's find out.

Lighthouse Leaders Hold the Vision

In section I, Brilliant Vision, we explored the power of creating a future so clear and compelling that others can't help but want to be part of it. But the work doesn't stop once the vision is crafted—the real leadership begins when you choose to carry that vision forward every day.

Lighthouse leaders rise to this challenge. They stand tall, unwavering, holding the light of the vision high above the storms and distractions that threaten to pull teams off course. When the path ahead grows murky, they shine clarity. When fear or fatigue creeps in, they radiate hope. Their steady presence reminds everyone: We have a destination. We have a purpose. We are moving forward, together.

You don't just announce a brilliant vision once and expect it to carry itself. You weave it into conversations, into priorities, into celebrations. You help each person see:
- where you are heading,
- why their work matters, and
- how they are an essential part of building that future.

Being a lighthouse leader means being the keeper of belief. You are the one who keeps the vision alive when others are tired, distracted, or unsure. You show them that even when the seas are rough, your light still shines—and you are still moving toward something extraordinary.

If you want to lead boldly, be the one who holds the light the highest—otherwise, the team will never see the shore. Be the leader who never lets it fade.

Linking Team to Vision and Goals—and to Each Other

True leadership connects people—not just to each other but to a shared vision of where they are headed. A team working toward a common goal cannot operate in siloes; they must be linked to the vision, the goals, and one another.

Just like the belay system for mountain climbing we talked about in chapter 2, the carabiners that secure each climber to the safety rope symbolize the connection to an organization's vision and goals. These links provide stability, direction, and trust. Like a lighthouse guiding ships to safe harbor, a strong belay system ensures that a team stays tethered to its purpose, even when the path is steep and uncertain.

Strengthening these connections requires more than setting direction; it demands real conversation. Asking probing questions and truly listening to your team builds the trust and clarity needed for a successful journey. Here are some questions you might consider using:

- What motivates you?
- How have you been motivated to achieve an essential goal in the past?
- What are your long-term goals?
- What does personal success look like for you?
- What does success mean to you in this role/in the organization?
- Where do you see alignment?
- Where is the disconnect?
- What might get in your way of achieving your goals?
- What are your ideas for overcoming the obstacles?

Expert tip: Remember to truly listen to their answers! Engagement will thrive when your team feels a deep connection not only to the mission and goals of their work but also to the leader who is supporting them.

Embracing Diverse Strengths

Today, diversity has become a charged topic in certain circles—but real leadership means rising above the noise.

True diversity goes far beyond race, gender, or any single characteristic. It embraces the full range of human difference: talents, skills, perspectives, lived experiences, and problem-solving approaches. When leaders intentionally build teams rich in diverse strengths and viewpoints, they create an environment where people are not only welcomed but also empowered to bring their best, most authentic selves to work every day.

This isn't about checking a box. It's about unlocking the full creative and performance potential of your team. When individuals feel seen, valued, and connected to a common purpose, they are more likely to lean into their strengths, think differently about challenges, and drive meaningful innovation. This is how bold organizations outperform, adapt faster, and win.

Rejecting diversity because of political discomfort is not only shortsighted; it's a leadership failure. Diversity of thought, experience, and strength has always been a catalyst for the greatest breakthroughs in history. Lighthouse leaders know this. They choose to lean in, not pull back.

You Don't Need (or Want) a Team of Clones

One of the most common traps that leaders fall into is assembling teams of people who look, think, and operate just like they do.

It feels comfortable—but it's dangerous.

Cloning yourself stifles creativity, narrows your field of vision, and leaves untapped talent and innovation on the sidelines.

Lighthouse leaders resist this trap. They actively seek out individuals with different strengths, perspectives, and life experiences. They know that true greatness isn't born from uniformity; it's forged from the powerful interplay of diverse voices, talents, and ideas working toward a shared goal.

The key is self-awareness.

Bold leaders recognize their own limitations and intentionally surround themselves with people who are stronger, smarter, and/or more capable in areas where they are not.

They don't feel threatened by excellence—they amplify it.

I've led many successful sales teams in the past, and every salesperson's approach to success was different. Some were more analytical and built beautiful spreadsheets with metrics and KPIs and used this impressive data to demonstrate the value of the solution to their clients. Others focused on active listening and building strong relationships with their clients. There is no one-size-fits-all or single way to achieve success; it's about recognizing, uplifting, and reinforcing what each person uniquely brings to the table. When team members are working in their "Zone of Genius," great things happen over and over again.

Zone of Genius

Dr. Gay Hendricks has explored how to spend more time living in our Zone of Genius—a term he coined—where creativity flows and there is exponential fulfillment and satisfaction. He has talked about the four zones in which we operate and how to move through them:

1. Zone of Incompetence: work we should stop doing
2. Zone of Competence: work we (but also others) do well
3. Zone of Excellence: work we perform at our best
4. Zone of Genius: work at the intersection of what we love and where we perform our best[xii]

Using this method can help lighthouse leaders ensure that their team members work in ways that make them not only happy but also highly effective.

Effective Feedback and Reinforcement

"I have some feedback for you." How do you typically react when you hear this statement?

"Uh oh!"

John Gottman's research highlights an important truth for leaders: the "magic ratio" for feedback is five positive comments for every one

119

criticism.[xiii] Without this balance, people tend to remember only the negative—and with it, lose momentum, confidence, and engagement.

BOLD leaders understand that feedback isn't just about correction. It's about reinforcement. It's about catching people doing things right and shining a light on the behaviors and contributions you want to see more of.

Praise should never be generic or automatic. It should be specific, personal, and deliberate, helping each individual see clearly what excellence looks like for them—and encouraging them to build on it.

Empty praise is noise. Intentional praise builds greatness.

Strong communication plays a vital role here. Remember the powerful principle: praise in public, correct in private. Every team member deserves to be held accountable with dignity, not humiliation. Accountability fuels growth, but mishandled feedback can fuel resentment and mistrust.

Leaders must be intentional in how recognition and redirection are distributed. Repeatedly singling out one individual—whether for criticism or praise—can make others feel unseen, undervalued, or sidelined. True leadership lifts the whole team. Find moments to celebrate and reinforce wins across every member of the team. Make it your mission to ensure that everyone feels seen, valued, and vital to the vision.

And when redirection is needed, make one-on-one coaching your superpower. Private conversations create safe spaces for honest feedback, courageous course corrections, and personal growth. They build trust, not fear—and turn feedback into a catalyst for continuous improvement. When leaders commit to feedback that uplifts, challenges, and grows people, they don't just shape better performance. They shape better leaders for the future.

You also want to be considerate of what you're recognizing. Take the following example.

A company kept finding itself in these "Hail Mary" moments—when everything seemed to be going downhill until someone saved the day at the last minute. At first, it was a thrill, like, "Wow, we pulled it off!" The leader even cheered on these moments, making it seem like they were the secret sauce to success.

But here's the kicker: relying on last-minute saves was like living on borrowed time. It gave the team a false sense that it was OK to stay focused in the present and keep doing things the way they had always been done because some were addicted to the adrenaline boost that came along with saving the day. Sure, it worked in the short run, but it burned everyone out.

The worst part? It kept the team stuck in a cycle of dealing with immediate fires, ignoring the bigger picture. While they were busy putting out flames, they missed out on making improvements and progress on the long-term goals that really mattered.

Let's be clear: there will always be moments that call for a Hail Mary—times when individuals must step up, adapt quickly, and manage through a crisis. But running a business by relying on constant heroics is not sustainable leadership. Fire drills should be the exception, not the operating model.

Strong leaders take a better approach. They address challenges early, celebrate the right behaviors, and build a culture focused on proactive collaboration and long-term goal achievement.

By consistently reinforcing positive actions—catching people doing things right and recognizing it—you minimize the need for last-minute rescues. You create an environment where teamwork, accountability, and steady progress are the norm, not the scramble.

The real heroes aren't the ones who save the day at the last minute. They're the ones who build systems, habits, and teams that make everyday success possible and reinforce them along the way.

Leading by Example: Actions over Words

One of the greatest responsibilities of leadership is to set the right example—not through speeches but through consistent, visible action. True leadership is not what you say; it's what you show.

Leading by example means aligning your words with your behavior every single day. It means rolling up your sleeves when needed and stepping into the work alongside your team—not to take over but to understand, guide, and inspire.

When leaders engage meaningfully without micromanaging, two powerful things happen:

- They gain a deeper understanding of the real challenges their teams face.
- They demonstrate humility and respect by showing that they aren't above hard work.

Finding the right balance is key. You don't do the work for them—that undermines growth and ownership. Instead, you model the spirit, attitude, and standards you want to see in them. You become the light they can follow, not the crutch they lean on.

Early in my career, I learned this lesson the hard way. I was often seen as the "go-to" person—the one who had all the answers and would far too often say, "Here, I'll do it. Just watch me."

At the time, I thought I was helping. But in reality, I was unintentionally limiting the very people I was trying to empower. By stepping in too quickly, I was sending a message: you're not capable.

Instead of building confidence, I was building dependency. Instead of creating space for them to grow, I was filling it myself.

Micromanagement doesn't just stifle creativity. It damages trust and morale. It sends a signal that the leader's way is the only way—ignoring the unique talents, approaches, and potential that each person brings.

Judith E. Glaser, in her book *Conversational Intelligence*, explains this perfectly. She found that when leaders tell someone exactly what to do, it spikes the listener's cortisol levels—they are actually increasing the stress hormones in the other person's body, feeling embarrassed or inadequate, or questioning their own competence. Either way, the result is the same: diminished engagement and trust. A better way? Lead through questions, not commands. Ask, guide, and empower your team to find their own best paths forward. Doing so stimulates positive neurotransmitters such as endorphins, building confidence, ownership, and genuine growth.

When we lead by example, we define the outcomes clearly—but we don't dictate every step.

We light the way, set the destination, and trust our people to navigate with their own strengths, creativity, and brilliance.

That's how leaders build not just strong teams but also stronger leaders for the future.

Remembering That Words Matter (Use Them Wisely)

"If I had more time, I would have written a shorter letter."
—Mark Twain

Far too often, leaders speak without fully considering the impact of their words—and regret it later. Though spontaneous speech sometimes has its place, off-the-cuff remarks can easily derail trust and momentum when not used thoughtfully.

The truth is that most leaders who seem to speak very effectively off the cuff have actually spent time carefully preparing for the moments that matter. Lighthouse leaders understand that words carry weight. They know that what they say can either ignite inspiration or cause unintended harm. They choose their words carefully—ensuring that their communication is respectful, supportive, and uplifting. They lead with empathy, actively listen first, and only speak after truly hearing others.

Expert tip: lighthouse leaders aim to be the last to speak, not the first.

At the core, people want to feel heard. They don't expect you to agree with everything they say, but they do expect you to value their voice. When team members feel listened to and respected, they are far more likely to be engaged, committed, and aligned with the vision.

One of the greatest acts of leadership—yet one that too few are willing to embrace—is taking full responsibility. A true lighthouse leader says, "If we succeed, it's because of my team. If we fail, it's because of me."

This mindset shines through in the way lighthouse leaders use words:

- They celebrate the team's collective achievements, not their own.
- They accept responsibility for missteps and protect their teams from blame.
- They recognize contributions across the team, creating a culture of shared ownership.

Together, we go farther. Together, we win.

Winning together isn't just about reaching goals; it's about creating meaning.

Employees today want more than a paycheck. They want to be part of something bigger.

They want to know that their work matters, that they belong, and that their voices are valued.

The most successful organizations understand this deeply. In businesses where owners and leaders intentionally foster the right culture, people stay—for 20 years or longer—not because they have to but because they want to. Because they are part of something that feels purposeful, connected, and real.

This is the essence of lighthouse leadership: guiding with words that build, not break—and creating a culture where everyone shines. Lighthouse leadership isn't about having all the answers or charging ahead alone; it's about consistently lighting the way for others. It's about holding the vision high, strengthening the connections between people and purpose, embracing the full spectrum of diverse strengths, and leading through intentional actions and words. When leaders embody the qualities of a lighthouse—clarity, consistency, humility, and courage—they don't just guide teams through calm seas; they help them navigate the storms. By building strong benches, amplifying strengths, reinforcing progress, and creating a culture of trust and shared ownership, lighthouse leaders enable their teams to go farther together than they ever could alone. In doing so, they don't just lead successful organizations; they build environments where people thrive, contribute meaningfully, and achieve extraordinary things.

BOLD Takeaways

- **Shine the vision bright and high.** Hold the vision steady through storms and distractions; your team needs to see the path ahead clearly in order to move forward confidently.

- **Build a connected and stronger team.** Strengthen the ties between your people, their work, and the vision. Encourage deep connection to the mission—and to one another.

- **Embrace strength in differences.** Don't build teams of clones. Seek out and amplify diverse strengths, perspectives, and approaches in order to create innovation, resilience, and lasting success.

- **Lead through action and integrity.** Your words and actions set the tone. Lead by example, take full responsibility, empower others to grow, and create a culture where every voice matters.

Chapter 9:
10-Minute Lighthouse Leadership Audit Exercise

Grab a notebook or open a blank document. Set a timer for 10 minutes and answer the following rapid-fire audit questions. Don't overthink—go with your first instinct!

1. Vision Check:

- Can every person on my team clearly describe where we are headed and why it matters?
                    (Yes/No/Not Sure)

2. Connection Check:

- How often do I have conversations that connect individuals back to our mission and to each other?
                    (Regularly/Occasionally/Rarely)

3. Strengths Check:

- Do I actively recognize and celebrate the unique strengths that each team member brings?
                    (Yes/Sometimes/No)

4. Diversity-of-Thinking Check:

- Am I encouraging a mix of voices, approaches, and perspectives in decision-making?
                    (Consistently/Sometimes/Not enough)

5. Communication Check:

- When giving feedback, do I lead with specific recognition before offering constructive input?
                    (Yes/Sometimes/No)

6. Ownership Check:

- Do I publicly give the team credit for wins and personally take responsibility for setbacks?
                    (Always/Sometimes/Rarely)

7. Leading-by-Example Check:

- When was the last time I modeled the behavior I expect from others?

    (This week/This month/Can't remember)

Reflection:

- Which areas are my biggest strengths right now?
- Which one area, if improved, would have the biggest positive impact on my team?
- What one action can I take this week to move closer to being the lighthouse leader my team deserves?

Chapter 10

Illuminate the Way

"Leadership is not about being in charge. It's about taking care of those in your charge."
—Simon Sinek

Lighthouse leadership is about illuminating the path for your team—keeping them focused on what needs to be accomplished and why it matters, and instilling the belief that success is possible. One of the most powerful ways to inspire and empower your team is by starting with the why. As Simon Sinek famously emphasized in his book Start with Why, the why connects people to a collective purpose and gives their work deeper meaning.[xiv] Without this clarity, teams will drift.

Lighthouse leaders use stories to bring the journey to life, strengthening connections and making the destination vivid and real. Purpose, passion, and hope are ignited through storytelling and story gathering—drawing from personal and professional experiences to create a vision that feels alive and achievable.

A perfect example comes from *The Wizard of Oz*. The movie famously begins in sepia tones, muted and dull. But at the 17-minute mark, Dorothy steps into a world of vibrant Technicolor, instantly drawing the viewer into the magic and wonder of Oz. Suddenly, everything feels possible. Everything feels worth striving for.

As leaders, we must do the same.

When we bring our brilliant vision to life in full Technicolor, we don't just inform minds—we awaken hearts. We help people see a future worth working toward and spark the hope that they can get there. The opportunity lies in painting a vivid, authentic picture—one rich in specifics, emotion, and meaning—so people feel connected to the purpose and believe in the path.

Here's the formula:

Start with *why* to unlock purpose and hope.

Then define the *what*: objectives, goals, and mission.

When leaders lead with vision, hope, and trust, they don't just drive results—they light a path that others are eager and inspired to follow.

Define the *What* by Setting Clear Goals

Once you have illuminated the *why*—the purpose and meaning behind the journey—the next essential move as a lighthouse leader is to define the *what*: the clear goals you are working toward together. Without clear goals, even the most inspired teams drift. The light becomes fuzzy. Momentum stalls. People lose sight of what matters most.

Clear goals turn purpose into action. They give your team a true destination to aim for—not just a feeling but a focus.

Why Clear Goals Matter

- **They create direction.**
  People can channel their energy toward what matters instead of scattering it across distractions.
- **They build confidence.**
  When people know exactly what success looks like, they can move forward with certainty instead of hesitation.
- **They strengthen accountability.**
  Clear goals make it easier to track progress, celebrate wins, and course-correct when necessary.
- **They foster motivation.**
  Progress is motivating. When people can see and measure how far they've come, they are more energized to keep moving forward.

Anchor Every Step in the Big Picture

Setting goals isn't just about getting things done; it's about making sure what gets done actually *matters*. The most effective leaders don't just check boxes—they choose goals that move the vision forward.

Remember the SMART framework from chapter 6? It gave you the structure: goals should be specific, measurable, achievable, relevant, and time-bound. Now it's time to elevate that structure by tying each goal back to the brilliant vision you're building.

Here's How to Do It:

1. Start with the vision

Before setting any goal, revisit your team or organizational vision. Ask:
- "What outcomes truly matter here?"
- "How will this goal get us closer to that future state?"

If a goal doesn't connect to the vision, it's a distraction—not a priority.

2. Make it personal and practical

Once you identify a vision-aligned area of focus, do the following:
- Use the SMART model to give the goal legs.
- Define what success looks like and when it will be achieved.
- Ensure that everyone understands the why behind the goal—not just the what.

Example:

Vision: Be the most trusted and responsive partner in our industry.

SMART goal: Reduce client response time from 12 hours to 2 hours by the end of Q3 by streamlining internal handoffs and introducing a shared inbox.

3. Link goals to meaning

Motivation increases when people see the impact of their work. Connect the dots for your team:

- "Here's how this goal supports our bigger purpose."
- "Here's how you're helping us become who we want to be."

This builds alignment, ownership, and accountability—the foundation of high performance.

Expert tip: Clarity beats complexity. Even the boldest vision can stall without clear, measurable goals. Keep connecting the everyday to the extraordinary. Example:

Sell more this year. (vague)

Increase client retention by 15 percent by Q4 by focusing on proactive communication strategies and articulating the value across our portfolio of services. (clear)

The Leader's Role: Keep the Goals Front and Center

Lighthouse leaders don't just set goals once and walk away. They keep the goals visible—like a lighthouse beam that sweeps across the horizon again and again. They:

- regularly remind the team of the what,
- tie everyday tasks back to the bigger goals,
- measure and communicate progress openly and often,
- celebrate milestones to keep the team energized and focused, and
- don't stop talking about the goals so that the team doesn't stop thinking about them.

Remember: Clarity isn't a one-time event; it's a continuous act of leadership.

Why "Vague Goals" Are a Hidden Danger

One of the biggest pitfalls that lighthouse leaders must avoid is setting vague, uninspiring goals.

When goals are unclear, teams make dangerous assumptions—or worse, disengage entirely.

A vague goal leaves your team wandering in the fog.

A clear goal becomes the North Star that keeps everyone aligned and moving forward.

Develop Your Leaders; Elevate Everyone

One of the most powerful ways to close the gap between where your organization is today and where you want it to be is by developing your people—especially your leaders. When leaders grow, everyone benefits.

Investing in leadership development creates a ripple effect. As leaders strengthen their skills, confidence, and capacity, they become better at supporting, guiding, and empowering others. Teams feel the difference. Performance improves. Culture improves. Innovation improves.

Everything moves forward when leaders do.

The best leaders also know this: people want to grow. They don't just want a paycheck—they want to be seen, valued, challenged, and developed. They want to know that they matter.

Gallup's research backs this up. In their well-known Q12 survey— the 12 elements that most powerfully drive employee engagement— several questions/statements focus directly on learning and growth, including rating the following statements on a scale from strongly agree to strongly disagree:

- "In the last year, I have had opportunities at work to learn and grow."
- "There is someone at work who encourages my development."

According to Gallup, organizations in which employees strongly agree with these statements consistently experience the following:

1. Higher productivity
2. Lower turnover
3. Greater profitability
4. Better customer satisfaction[xv]

When people feel like others are invested in them, they engage more fully. When they feel stagnant or overlooked, they disengage—and often, they leave. Developing your leaders isn't a luxury—it's a strategic imperative. It sends these signals to your people:

- *You matter.*
- *We believe in your potential.*
- *We are building the future together.*

Leadership development isn't about fixing people; it's about unlocking their strengths, expanding their impact, and lighting the way for others to follow.

The truth is simple: Grow your leaders. Grow your business. Grow your future.

Hirewell is a leading talent-acquisition and recruiting firm based in Chicago, known for its modern, consultative approach to hiring. To accelerate the company's growth, CEO Matt Massucci identified three key priorities:

1. Develop leaders to expand their scope and scale the business
2. Strengthen strategic thinking
3. Build executive presence

As we crafted the action plan, we started where it mattered most: developing his leaders. That's because when leaders grow, everything else—strategic thinking, executive presence, and business scale—follows more naturally.

Our first step was helping his leaders craft a brilliant vision for success, then teaching them to communicate it clearly and consistently through lighthouse leadership.

Many of these leaders had been high-performing player/coaches, leaning heavily on "doing" rather than empowering others and helping their team members learn. They were used to achieving success by rolling up their sleeves and doing it themselves, but as the company grew, that approach was becoming a bottleneck.

We shifted the focus. Developing and empowering Hirewell's teams became a top priority, not an afterthought.

- Leaders began lifting their heads to think more strategically.
- They spent more time coaching and less time doing.
- Teams became more engaged, more capable, and more aligned to the bigger vision.

When leaders step into lighthouse leadership—guiding the way rather than carrying all the weight—everyone rises.

Tell, Don't Show

Writers are taught to show, not tell. But in lighthouse leadership, the opposite is true: tell, don't show.

As leaders, it's our job to make sure the *what*—the goal, the mission, the destination—is absolutely clear. But when we overstep and control the *how*—getting into the details of the way the team should do the work—even with the best intentions, we undermine trust and motivation. Micromanagement is consistently ranked as one of employees' top frustrations. Yet most leaders don't intend to micromanage—they believe "showing how it's done" will be faster, more efficient, and helpful. They justify it as "leading by example."

When you step in and say, "Let me do it," here's what your team actually hears:

- "I don't trust you to do it right."
- "I don't believe you can handle it on your own."

The result?

Demotivation. Resentment. And eventually, learned helplessness—where team members stop trying altogether and just wait for the leader to take over.

Leaders often feel enormous pressure to have all the answers. But the truth is that your team doesn't need another pair of hands—they need a sounding board, a coach, and a champion. They need you to ask great questions, not give them your answers.

Why? Because your way might not be their way. Each person has different strengths, experiences, and problem-solving styles. Your job is to help them find the solution that works best for them—not force them to mirror you.

Instead of telling, ask the following:

- "When faced with a similar challenge, what worked for you before?"
- "What options do you have?"
- "What does success look like in this situation?"
- "Where are you feeling stuck?"

Expert tip: the best leaders don't have the best answers—they ask the best questions.

When you lead with curiosity, you help your team self-discover the best path forward. You unlock their creativity, their confidence, and their ownership. Whether someone's strength is relationship building, data analysis, or creative problem-solving, the goal is to leverage what they do best, not override it.

Because the greatest growth—and the greatest wins—happen when people find their own way forward.

By asking the right questions, you are helping your team discover their answers—the ones that will work best for them. Everyone has their strengths and ways of doing things. Your questions should help your team self-discover their best course of action for their *how* in response to your *what* and *why*. For example, if someone is great at relationship building, their solution will likely lean into that. Or if they are good at data, it may be putting together a plan that yields an incredible ROI that will help the client see the value. The point is that we should be leveraging these strengths for the team's betterment, not ignoring them so we can do it all by ourselves.

Asking such questions as, "What are your thoughts on how you could proceed?" "What have you tried so far?" "How have you solved a problem such as this in the past?" "What would a great outcome be in solving this problem/achieving this goal?" and "What does success look like?" are ways to help your employees self-discover their best answers. They will be more successful because they will move forward in a way that matches their strengths. We've compiled a great list of questions and posted them for your reference on our website at www.aspirationcatalyst.com/boldleadershipresources.

Leverage Strengths, Minimize Weaknesses

Once you've asked the right questions and received answers from the team, you better understand each member's strengths and weaknesses. Remember the CliftonStrengths assessment from Oneness? It's a valuable tool for quickly identifying your team members' strengths, enabling you to empower them more effectively. By focusing on their strengths, you can effectively guide them toward success.

Consider these questions: *How could they accomplish the job using their strengths? How could they approach the task in a way that leverages their talents? If they have a weakness in a necessary area, how can they use another strength or find a partner to help?* Usually, team members can perform their duties using their inherent strengths and talents. After all, their competency is why they were hired in the first place. It often comes down to the *how*. There are multiple ways to achieve goals based on an individual's natural inclinations. Leveraging their strengths helps uncover these alternative methods.

I had the opportunity to work with a highly talented sales director named Kurt, who was underutilized in ways that mattered most. Kurt's natural strength was strategic thinking. He could see patterns, anticipate market shifts, and develop forward-looking solutions that could position our team ahead of competitors. But despite this gift, Kurt had never been invited into strategic conversations. His role, like so many mid-level leaders, was narrowly defined around execution: drive the sales numbers, manage the pipeline, keep the machine running.

It was a missed opportunity—not just for Kurt but for the entire organization.

When I started working with him, I immediately saw the gap. Here was someone who didn't just want to "make the number"—he wanted to help shape the future. I made it a priority to invite Kurt into strategy discussions—first informally, then more formally in broader leadership meetings. His insights opened new pathways we hadn't considered before—and our overall strategy got better because of it.

It wasn't just about giving Kurt a "seat at the table." It was about recognizing and activating a strength that had been overlooked—and showing him that his contributions mattered beyond quota reports and dashboards.

At the end of the day, empowering Kurt didn't just elevate him; it elevated our entire team.

When you unleash someone's true strengths, you don't just improve performance. You create loyalty. You build belief. You transform what's possible.

This example shows that understanding the difference between team members' strengths and weaknesses is one of the most important jobs of a leader. Most of the time, it's not about moving them around from role to role but rather helping them leverage their strengths effectively in their current role. You can only develop and empower your team if you know how they work best. It's the only way to keep moving up and have a bigger impact.

"True leadership is when people follow you when they have a choice not to."
—Jim Collins

Motivation

People need to believe they have a **real chance to win**. That means the leader must be credible—and so must the goal. When we rally teams around a common purpose, our Brilliant Vision has to clearly define what winning looks like and what it will take to get there.

Whether it's achieving a specific revenue target by a set date or completing a project on time, a well-defined goal keeps everyone's eyes on the prize and drives collective effort. Progress must be measured and reported with transparency so the team always knows where they stand.

Along the way, celebrating small wins builds momentum, keeps energy high, and reinforces the sense of accomplishment. Consistent communication and visibility are what sustain engagement, ensuring that people stay motivated and aligned as they work together toward the common goal.

Princeton began his life as a relatively unimpressive racehorse but was then transitioned to an OTTB (off-the-track thoroughbred), which means he was retired from racing to begin a new career as a hunter/jumper show horse. The horse knew how to run fast and safely without injury but had zero training in jumping.

Remember the saying, "You can lead a horse to water but can't make it drink"? The same is valid for training them. You can't get them to do what you want without a lot of time, patience, positive reinforcement, and repetition.

Before we talk about training, you should know that adult horses weigh an average of 1,000 pounds and are prey animals, so flight is their primary method of survival. They are highly perceptive and sensitive.

Princeton's trainer started from the very beginning to teach the horse his new craft. She utilized concrete, incremental goals, rewards, and a lot of practice and praise. The horse was connected to a long lunge rope and quickly learned simple commands such as walk, trot, and canter. Eventually, he walked over ground poles and jumped smaller fences. Princeton quickly understood and received positive reinforcement each time he did the right thing. Next, a rider climbed onto the saddle to teach the horse to pay attention to leg signals versus voice commands. Over time, with abundant positive reinforcement and patience, the rider and horse jumped beautifully together.

They could focus on improving technique and speed, leading to winning performances on the equestrian circuit.

Unfortunately, this approach is the opposite of what leaders do when expecting high performance from their employees and teams. In the above scenario, if we applied the typical training techniques employed by a corporate leader, the horse would be expected to jump without much training and without the incremental goals to teach, breed confidence, and build success. This approach is a recipe for frustration and failure. But, as with Princeton, we can see that there are certain actions a leader can take.

Setting clear expectations and guiding your team through the necessary steps are essential for creating lasting behavior change. Small wins add up to big victories. By focusing on incremental progress and celebrating achievements, you build momentum, boost confidence, and reinforce the behaviors that drive success.

The collective results are extraordinary when every team member consistently exhibits the right behaviors. High performance becomes the norm, not the exception.

People naturally want to be part of a winning team.

It feels good to contribute, to grow, and to be part of something larger than themselves.

And as an added bonus? When people feel connected to a shared success, they perform at even higher levels—again and again.

Illuminate the Way...and Keep Illuminating It

Every leader strives for high team performance—but not all succeed.

Take Princeton, our beautiful, once-untrained striking chestnut thoroughbred, as an example of what true high-level performance looks like. We had a clear vision for his success and knew it would take time, focus, and consistent effort to achieve it. In his early years, Princeton learned only how to run as fast as possible around a track. His new role required him to compete in equestrian competitions with both intelligence and grace. This transformation is a perfect illustration of change management in the equestrian world—and mirrors the kind of change we guide our teams through.

A few years later, Princeton completed a third-round jump-off at an equestrian competition, effortlessly clearing a complex series of jumps in perfect sync with his rider. Their winning round looked smooth and easy—but behind that "effortlessness" was years of dedication and hard work.

How did this beautiful horse and its rider achieve such a high level of performance?

Through deliberate training, continuous reinforcement, patience, and time.

And that's the leadership lesson: illuminating the path is not a one-time act. It requires consistent guidance, support, and communication throughout the journey—not just shining a light at the starting line and walking away.

Clear Communication Is Continuous Communication

One of the biggest mistakes leaders make is to assume that saying something once is sufficient. It makes sense in their own mind as they've spent time thinking it through. But then the team only hears it once for the first time, often without the same context or depth. The same applies to leadership communication: if you want your message to stick, you have to repeat it—clearly and consistently.

The Rule of Seven in marketing states that people typically need to hear a message at least seven times in order to truly absorb and act on it.

- **Without repetition, even the best ideas get lost in the noise.**
  Effective leaders understand that communication isn't about making a statement; it's about building understanding.
- **And it's not just about frequency; it's about format.**
  Whether it's a town-hall meeting, an email, a one-on-one conversation, or a whiteboard in the office, the message needs to

stay front and center in ways that the team can easily see and internalize.

- **If something important is mentioned once and never reinforced, most people will just default back to what they've always done.**

They aren't being resistant—they simply don't know any better.

- **No news isn't good news in leadership.**

Too often, it means a missed opportunity.

A Simple (and Funny) Reminder

Think about it this way: if one partner said to the other, "I told you I loved you when we got married—if anything changes, I'll let you know," we'd laugh at how ridiculous that sounds.

The same is true for your team!

They need to hear the message often:

- "Where are we going?"
- "Why does it matter?"
- "What's at stake if we don't succeed?"

The light must stay lit—and visible.

Clear leadership is not a one-time event—it's a continuous act of illuminating the path, reinforcing direction, and staying present for your team. Like Princeton's journey from an untrained racehorse to a high-performing show jumper, achieving excellence requires more than a clear starting point; it demands deliberate training, consistent encouragement, and visible leadership every step of the way. Lighthouse leaders know that without consistent communication, even the best goals lose their power. By keeping the light on—clarifying the vision, reinforcing key messages, and guiding teams through change—we create the conditions for long-term trust, growth, and high performance. Leadership is not just about setting the course; it's about walking it with your team—with patience, persistence, and purpose.

BOLD Takeaways

- **Illuminate the way—consistently.** Leadership requires continuously shining a light on the path forward, not just pointing it out once.

- **Communicate with clarity and care.** Teams need to hear important messages multiple times and through different channels in order to fully align and stay engaged.

- **Progress requires repetition.** Just as deliberate training leads to high performance, consistent leadership and communication build momentum and confidence and yield results.

- **Trust is built through presence.** Staying visible and accessible and reinforcing the vision are good ways to earn lasting trust and commitment from your team.

Chapter 10:
Illuminate the Way Journal Prompts

Instructions

Great leaders don't just charge forward—they illuminate the path. Use this journal to reflect on how clearly you're communicating the *why*, setting goals that matter, and helping your team move forward with clarity and confidence. Come back to these prompts anytime you need to refocus, realign, or reignite your leadership light.

1. Reconnect to the *why.*
Prompt: What is the bigger purpose behind our work—and have I clearly shared it? Where might my team be unclear or disconnected from that purpose?

2. Identify what's in the fog.
Prompt: Where am I shining the light effectively—and where might it be dim? What's one key message or goal I need to reinforce this week?

3. Bridge the day-to-day to the vision.
Prompt: How often do I tie small actions back to our bigger mission? What habits or rhythms could help me do this more consistently?

4. Tell a story that inspires.
Prompt: What story am I telling—and is it creating belief? What moment or metaphor could bring our journey to life?

5. Ask, don't tell.
Prompt: Where am I overdirecting instead of empowering? What's one powerful question I could ask instead of jumping in?

6. Activate strengths instead of overlooking them.
Prompt: Whose strengths on my team am I underutilizing? How can I help them use those strengths more effectively this week?

7. Reinforce the message.
Prompt: Have I communicated our key goals clearly—and often enough? What channels or rituals could help me repeat and reinforce them?

8. Make success visible.
Prompt: Have I defined what success looks like—for me and the team? Is it clear, motivating, and measurable?

9. Celebrate momentum.
Prompt: What small wins can I highlight right now? How can I use recognition to energize the team?

10. Define the leader you're becoming.
Prompt: What do I want my team to say about my leadership? What actions am I taking—or avoiding—that shape that narrative?

Lead with Listening

"The art of communication is the language of leadership."
—James C. Humes

Communication isn't just talking; it's the lifeline that turns vision into reality.

As leaders, it's easy to think that our job is done once we've shared a plan, set a goal, or explained a strategy. But real leadership communication doesn't stop at speaking; it begins with ensuring that the message is received, understood, and embraced. If it isn't understood, it doesn't exist.

Communication is the thread that weaves ideas into action. It creates the space where trust is built, innovation flourishes, and alignment is achieved. Without it, even the clearest vision will falter.

In lighthouse leadership, communication isn't a one-time announcement or a one-way street but rather an ongoing, two-way dialogue that strengthens connection, inspires ownership, and lights the path forward.

Effective Communication Is a Two-Way Street

Communication also isn't just broadcasting information; it's creating a bridge between people. It's not enough to share announcements or updates. True communication invites dialogue, questions, input, and feedback. It's a conversation, not a monologue.

Lighthouse leaders know that effective communication flows both ways. It's not about commanding or controlling the narrative; it's about opening the door wide enough for others to step through and contribute. When leaders invite and encourage real dialogue, they gain access to richer ideas, deeper perspectives, and stronger team commitment.

The best leaders don't just talk at their teams—they engage with them. They create environments where people feel safe to share their thoughts, challenge ideas respectfully, and offer feedback without fear of retribution. They foster a climate where curiosity, not compliance, leads the way.

BOLD Rule of Lighthouse Leadership: Listen First, Speak Last

When leaders rush to be the first voice in the room, they unintentionally shut down discussion. People start to think, Why bother sharing? The decision's already made.

But when leaders hold back, when they ask great questions and truly listen, they show their teams that every voice matters. That's when the magic happens. That's when teams become more engaged, more creative, and more committed.

It takes humility to truly listen. It takes courage to invite perspectives you may not have considered. But it is in this two-way flow that leadership transforms from directing people to inspiring them.

If you want your communication to move hearts and minds, don't just deliver the message—create the conversation.

Press 1 If You're Missing the Point

Earlier in my career, while leading a sales team, I learned a valuable lesson about the importance of communicating the *why* behind our actions. We were tasked with boosting productivity and noticed a growing reliance on email as a crutch. From experience, we knew that increased phone activity typically led to higher sales, so we devised what we thought was a brilliant plan: a contest. The idea was simple.

Whichever team logged the most call time and number of calls would win a prize. It seemed like a foolproof strategy. *What could possibly go wrong?*

At first, the results were promising. Call times and the number of calls increased, and I felt good about our initiative. But something was off: revenue wasn't increasing as expected. This contradicted the very purpose of the contest. Curious, I decided to listen in on some of the calls to see if there was a need for additional training.

The first call I listened to began with, "Welcome to Moviefone."

It was followed by a long recording of the day's movie times at a local theater. I fast-forwarded, only to hear the same recording again. Baffled, I checked another salesperson's call. "Welcome to Moviefone" echoed once more. After the third instance, I knew something was seriously wrong.

I approached the team leader and asked if she was aware that her team was calling Moviefone all day. To my surprise, she proudly admitted that not only was she aware but she had actually recommended it as a clever way to increase call time and win the contest. I was stunned.

After pausing for a moment, I asked her, "Why do you think we wanted more calls in the first place?"

Without hesitation, she answered, "To win the contest."

I pressed further, "But why did we create the contest? What was the real goal behind it?"

She paused, thinking it over, and then admitted, "I'm not sure."

Realizing that her intentions were good, I had to reflect on my role. I explained that the real objective of the contest was not simply to increase call time but rather to be on the phone with clients to foster deeper relationships and gather insights to drive more sales. She was genuinely remorseful, but I knew the fault lay with me. As a leader, I was responsible for ensuring that everyone understood not just the what but also the why behind our strategies.

This experience taught me a crucial lesson: communicating the rationale behind decisions is vital for ensuring alignment and success. From then on, I vowed never to overlook the importance of explaining the why to my team and ensuring that they understood.

Make the Mission Matter

If you want people to care, you have to show them why it matters. Clear, transparent communication isn't just about sharing tasks or timelines; it's about connecting the work to a deeper purpose. When teams understand the why behind what they're doing, their energy shifts. They move from compliance to commitment, from merely showing up to stepping up.

Imagine launching a new product line without explaining its impact. Team members would likely stick to their old routines, missing the urgency to adapt. But when you connect the dots—how it serves clients better, strengthens the company, and creates new opportunities—suddenly, the change has meaning. Now they're not just doing a job—they're building something bigger than themselves.

If the vision feels vague or uninspiring, don't expect passion or progress. People won't fight for a goal they don't understand or believe in. Over the years, we've learned this simple truth: the more vivid, meaningful, and exciting you make the vision, the more people will want to be part of it.

Spell out what success looks like. Share why it matters. Then ask your team, "How can we help each other get there?"

When the *why* is strong, the *how* becomes unstoppable.

When the Beacon Fades

At a high-performing technology company I worked for, there was a powerful motivator every employee could see each day: the Customer Loyalty Meter. Every time we logged into our computers, we were reminded of the high percentage of truly loyal clients we had earned—an achievement we all took pride in. It connected everyone's daily work to a bigger mission: serving customers and making a difference.

Then came the acquisition. After two private-equity firms bought the company, the focus subtly but significantly shifted—from customers to EBITDA, the financial metric that measures profitability as a percentage of revenue. Shortly after the acquisition, I went on maternity leave. When I returned, I was stunned to see the Customer Loyalty Meter replaced by a new dashboard: the EBITDA Meter.

The problem?

As I said on Page 7, most employees didn't know what EBITDA was, let alone how they could influence it. And frankly, why would they? EBITDA mattered enormously to the investors—but it wasn't a lighthouse for the team. It wasn't something they could connect to, get excited about, or feel ownership over.

The result was predictable: confusion, disengagement, and, eventually, higher turnover.

Now, don't get me wrong—measuring EBITDA is critical for owners, boards, and executives. But it's not the right way to rally your team. If you want to inspire people, you have to connect them to something they can feel and influence. Replacing a customer-centered beacon with an abstract financial metric dimmed the light that had once guided the organization's success.

A lighthouse leader knows: if the path isn't clear and meaningful, people lose their way.

Communication and Building Authentic Relationships

In today's competitive landscape, the war for talent is fierce. People want to know that their leaders genuinely care about them. No one wants to feel like mere cogs in a wheel—they want recognition and a true connection. To give them that, we need to be intentional and forward-thinking about maintaining regular communication, especially in the absence of face-to-face interactions.

> *"People don't care how much you know until they know how much you care."*
> —Theodore Roosevelt

I often look at it through the lens of communication because doing so highlights the importance of empathy and genuine concern in building relationships and earning trust. To win people over, more than possessing knowledge or expertise is required. Your team needs to feel valued, heard, and understood on a personal level. In other words, in lighthouse leadership, we need to demonstrate compassion and show that we genuinely care about their well-being. This is a golden opportunity for communication.

For many, it used to be far easier to build this trust and rapport. We had more opportunities to do so in an office setting. We would walk to the conference room with a team member and ask how their weekend was, what was new with their kids, and other questions that were more personal in nature and helped us build stronger relationships. Even these simple questions within 5 to 10 minutes helped to establish a deeper connection. But today, we jump on a Zoom call and often get right down to business, then we end the call and move on to whatever is next. In so doing, we're missing out on opportunities to connect without those casual interactions that occurred naturally in an office setting. This is why lighthouse leaders are intentional about deepening these relationships. They consistently engage in regular conversations with their team members and establish a communication cadence that keeps everyone informed and aligned.

One of our preferred frameworks for doing this comes from Gallup's book *It's the Manager* by Jim Clifton and Jim Harter.[xvi] They highlight the "Five Conversations That Drive Performance," a framework based on research into the practices of the best managers. These five conversations include the following:

- Clarifying roles, goals, and expectations to ensure that everyone understands their responsibilities
- 10-minute quick connects to check in on progress and provide immediate reinforcement
- 30-minute check-ins to celebrate wins and align on goals and progress
- Developmental coaching, often referred to as feedback, to support continuous growth
- Career progress reviews to focus on long-term development and aspirations[xvii]

These conversations strike a balance between short-term needs and long-term goals, ensuring that communication between the leader and employee remains regular and productive. Pick the framework that works best for you and stick to it. Consistency in communication is most important.

Impact on Trust

Trust is the bedrock of both relationships and lighthouse leadership. Though clear, regular, and transparent communication is essential to building trust, maintaining it requires ongoing effort and consistency. Consider this example: During the early stages of the pandemic, a leader stopped holding one-on-one meetings with a key team member. Initially, this might have seemed understandable, given the significant adjustments everyone was making in an unprecedented time. However, when these meetings ceased for six months, the employee—vital to the team—began feeling isolated and uncertain about her direction and goals. Eventually, she left the role. What had initially been a dream job turned into a nightmare due to an unsupportive and uncommunicative leader.

Trust can also be eroded by not just the absence of communication but also the wrong type of communication—such as when team members believe a leader is talking about them behind their back. If a leader gains a reputation for gossiping or spreading rumors—even seemingly minor ones—it can quickly undermine their authenticity. People naturally begin to wonder, *What are they saying about me?*

Lighthouse leaders avoid such behavior. They understand the importance of listening more and speaking less, reinforcing positive behaviors and accomplishments. By recognizing and praising individuals for their contributions and progress, leaders can motivate and inspire their teams to continue striving for excellence.

Expert tip: focus on uplifting others through guidance and support.

A coach once shared with me a powerful way to think before speaking: "If you were on *60 Minutes*, would you be proud of how you're showing up right now? Does what you're saying need to be said, and in this manner?"

This perspective encourages leaders to communicate with integrity and thoughtfulness, ensuring that their words build trust rather than erode it.

Lighthouse leaders focus on consistently uplifting others with guidance and support. They understand the importance of listening more, speaking less, and reinforcing positive behaviors and accomplishments. By acknowledging and praising individuals for their contributions and progress, providing critical feedback when needed in a supportive manner, leaders motivate and inspire their team members to continue striving for excellence.

Listen First, Speak Last

Regardless of the situation, we all want to feel heard. It's human nature—and our teams are no different. Allowing someone to feel heard starts with active listening, asking the right questions, and—remember this if you remember nothing else—leaders speaking last.

Rather than dominating conversations with their thoughts and opinions, lighthouse leaders prioritize active listening. This approach allows team members to feel valued and heard while you continue to build strong relationships by better understanding the needs and perspectives of others. It involves fully engaging in the conversation, paying attention to verbal and nonverbal cues, and demonstrating genuine interest in what the other person is saying.

When we do this, we are also more likely to ask the right questions. It's important to remember that the best leaders don't necessarily have the best answers, but they do have the best questions.

They excel at asking thought-provoking and open-ended queries that help others come up with their own solutions. They encourage dialogue and create space for the team members to express themselves. Think of it this way: the goal as a lighthouse leader is to become the chief listening/question officer.

You might be thinking that, with all this emphasis on listening, there is little room for talking. And you're right. There's a common misconception that leaders should dominate discussions. In reality, effective leaders facilitate discussions by asking thoughtful questions and holding back their opinions until later. By refraining from immediately sharing their own ideas or dictating how tasks should be accomplished, leaders create space for team members to contribute their perspectives. When leaders speak first, team members often feel compelled to align with the leader's views, believing that the decision has already been made. This approach can inadvertently stifle valuable insights and diverse viewpoints.

The real goal is to encourage your team to speak up. Though you are the person who's illuminating the path, they are the ones traversing it. They are intimate with the terrain and often have a unique and more detailed perspective, whether it's understanding what customers truly want or identifying the challenges faced in operations. Since they are closest to the work, they frequently have ideas that are more insightful and practical than our own. If we constantly direct the conversation with our own thoughts, team members may stop offering their input, feeling like they're just being told what to do.

As a lighthouse leader, it's crucial to demonstrate that you value your team's contributions and creativity. If team members feel like they only ever receive instructions without the chance to add value or share their ideas, they are likely to become disengaged. Instead, focus on creating a collaborative environment where everyone's ideas are heard and appreciated. This approach fosters engagement and leads to more innovative and effective solutions.

Communication When It's Difficult

Despite our best intentions, conflict is inevitable—and that's not always a bad thing. When we are working hard to achieve big visions and important goals, emotions can run high. Productive conflict, when handled well, can lead to stronger teams, smarter solutions, and deeper trust. When conflict arises, lighthouse leaders take a direct and proactive approach—but not by playing referee. Our job isn't to fix the problem for them; it's to empower team members to navigate challenges independently, build resilience, and strengthen relationships.

If someone approaches you about a conflict, your first question should always be, "What steps have you taken to address it?"

Encourage them to engage directly with the other person and resolve the issue within 24 hours if possible. You can offer support—through role-playing, brainstorming approaches, or helping them script a difficult conversation—but they must take the lead. For accountability, ask them to follow up with you after the conversation has taken place.

When leaders jump in and mediate every issue, they unintentionally weaken trust between team members. When we empower individuals to handle conflict themselves, we build a culture of ownership, courage, and mutual respect.

Feedback Is the Fuel for Growth

Often, conflict stems from feedback—or the lack of it. As people grow in their careers, feedback becomes less frequent, even though their impact only increases. That's a dangerous combination.

Lighthouse leaders foster a feedback-rich environment by both giving and receiving feedback with humility and gratitude.

As Kim Scott shares in *Radical Candor*, the key is balancing two essentials: caring personally and challenging directly.[xviii]

And as Brené Brown wisely reminds us in *Dare to Lead*, "There is no mastery without feedback. But it's hard. My mantra for receiving feedback: Be brave. Listen. Take what's helpful and leave the rest. My mantra for giving feedback: Clear is kind. Unclear is unkind."[xix]

Read the Room—and Listen to What's Unspoken

Effective communication goes far beyond words. Lighthouse leaders are deeply attuned to the undercurrents in a conversation:

- What's being said?
- What's not being said?
- Where might fear, uncertainty, or frustration be hiding?

By listening between the lines, leaders can uncover underlying concerns, address root issues early, and guide conversations back toward alignment and positive action. If someone veers off track—or exhibits behavior that undermines the team's goals—your role is to gently, but clearly, redirect them. Offer constructive feedback, reinforce the bigger vision, and always assume positive intent.

Bottom Line

When handled well, conflict doesn't break teams. It builds them. It creates the opportunity for clarity, growth, and stronger trust—that is, if leaders have the courage to guide, not fix.

In lighthouse leadership, communication isn't a broadcast; it's a bridge. It's not enough to simply send messages out. Leaders must ensure that their communication is understood and trusted and invites genuine dialogue. True communication inspires connection, builds trust, and lights the way forward. When leaders actively listen, clarify the why, and create conversation space, they unlock their team's full power. From everyday interactions to navigating conflict, effective communication is the thread that weaves together vision, trust, ownership, and progress. Great leadership begins not with talking but with listening—and with making every conversation a catalyst for alignment, engagement, and growth.

BOLD Takeaways

- **Bridge the gap.** Communication isn't complete when you speak; it's complete when your team understands. Focus on clarity, meaning, and ensuring that the message connects.

- **Open the door.** Make communication a two-way street. Create space for dialogue, invite feedback, and show your team that every voice matters.

- **Listen first, speak last.** Hold back your opinions. Listen deeply, ask thoughtful questions, and empower your team to think, contribute, and own the path forward.

- **Defuse and develop.** When conflict arises, coach your team to handle it directly, to seek feedback bravely, and to grow stronger together. Conflict handled well builds trust, not division.

Chapter 11:
Lead with Listening Journal Prompts

Great leaders don't just talk—they listen, connect, and clarify. Use this journal to reflect on your communication habits, your team's understanding, and your ability to create space for dialogue. Revisit these prompts regularly to stay aligned, build trust, and lead with intention.

1. How clearly have I communicated the *why* behind our current priorities?
Where might I assume that people understand the purpose when in fact they may not?

2. Am I creating space for dialogue or just delivering updates?
What opportunities have I provided this week for my team to share, question, or contribute?

3. Do I truly listen or just wait to speak?
When was the last time I let others speak first and shaped my response based on what I heard?

4. Where might miscommunication or vagueness be slowing us down?
What message or expectation do I need to clarify immediately?

5. When have I recently explained the *why* behind a decision?
How did my team respond, and what can I learn from that?

6. How intentional have I been about building connection—not just communicating information?
What small personal interactions have helped me build trust this week?

7. Am I recognizing nonverbal cues and what's not being said?
Where might someone on my team be holding back, disengaged, or misunderstood?

8. Have I encouraged healthy conflict and direct feedback?
What questions can I ask in order to normalize open dialogue and avoid avoidance?

9. How am I showing my team that their voices matter?

What specific actions or behaviors demonstrate that I value their input?

10. What will I do this week to become a better listener?

What mindset or habit can I adopt in order to lead with greater clarity and care?

People First

"If you're going to live, leave a legacy. Make a mark on the world that can't be erased."
—Maya Angelou

It's difficult to talk about lasting impact without also talking about legacy. The two are very closely intertwined with a common denominator being the impact that our presence makes after we are no longer physically present. Legacy is defined as "something transmitted by or received from an ancestor or predecessor from the past."[xx] Much like how the term often comes up when we talk about death, think of it as an opportunity to be intentional about the mark we are leaving and to take the proper actions to make sure we are remembered as we wish to be.

People First vs. Profit Focused

For leaders, legacy isn't about the titles held or the profits posted; it's about the imprint we leave on others after we've moved on. It's the story that others tell when we're no longer in the room. It's the value that endures because we built up something—and someone—stronger than before.

The real questions are these:
- How will you be remembered?
- What will continue growing long after your name is removed from the org chart?
- Will your impact be something sustainable, uplifting, and meaningful?

In my experience, extraordinary things happen when leaders focus on people first. They leave others better than they found them. They ignite a ripple effect that reaches far beyond their immediate circle, equipping people to lift others too.

If I could choose how my leadership is remembered, I wouldn't want a statue in the lobby or my name on a plaque. I'd want the real monument to be the people I helped grow—the lives I touched, the leaders I inspired, and the confidence I helped spark. For me, that's the kind of legacy worth striving for.

Yet even with the best of intentions, many celebrated leaders lose sight of this. Some become so consumed with strategy, operations, products, or profits that they forget the people who fuel them.

Take Jack Welch, the legendary CEO of General Electric (GE), often hailed as a business titan. Under his leadership, GE's market value sky-rocketed from $12 billion to over $400 billion in the span of 20 years. Revenues and profits soared. Welch's emphasis on performance, accountability, and operational excellence was transformative.

But there was another side. His relentless short-term focus—through tactics such as aggressive stock buybacks and the infamous "rank and yank" employee-evaluation system—created a cutthroat culture. It boosted earnings temporarily and eroded long-term trust, morale, and sustainability.

By 2021, GE—once a symbol of American industrial greatness—had been broken into three smaller companies. Some would argue that the empire Welch built didn't endure because of the short-term wins that came at the expense of lasting impact.

Was Welch a BOLD leader? Not by our definition. BOLD leaders balance performance with people. They understand that sustainable success isn't built on fear or short-term gains; it's built on trust, empowerment, and collective strength.

And the evidence backs it up: putting people first isn't just the right thing to do; it's the smart thing to do.

(Don't just take my word for it—I'll show you the proof.)

The Proof Point of People-First Leadership

The principle of prioritizing people over profits can be demonstrated through several key outcomes, supported by research and real-world examples:

1. **Higher Employee Engagement and Productivity**

   Organizations that invest in their people see higher levels of employee engagement, which translates into increased productivity. Engaged employees are more motivated, take ownership of their work, and are willing to go the extra mile.

   Proof: Gallup research shows that businesses with high employee engagement are 21 percent more profitable and 17 percent more productive.

2. **Lower Turnover and Retention of Top Talent**

   Focusing on people leads to lower turnover rates, as employees feel valued, supported, and loyal to the organization. Retaining top talent reduces costs associated with hiring and training new employees.

   Proof: A study by the Work Institute finds that turnover costs companies over $600 billion annually, and creating a people-centered culture reduces this expense significantly.

3. **Enhanced Customer Satisfaction and Loyalty**

   When employees are well-treated, they are more likely to deliver better customer service, which leads to higher customer satisfaction, loyalty, and repeat business. Happy employees create happy customers.

   Proof: Harvard Business Review reports that companies with highly engaged employees have 10-percent higher customer ratings and show a 20-percent increase in sales.

4. **Innovation and Growth**

When people are put first, organizations foster a culture of trust, inclusion, and collaboration, which drives innovation and creativity. Employees are more likely to contribute ideas and help the company grow.

Proof: Research by MIT finds that companies that prioritize psychological safety and employee well-being see a significant increase in innovation and long-term growth.

5. **Long-Term Profitability**

Though prioritizing people may seem like a trade-off against profits in the short term, companies that focus on people first often outperform their competitors over the long term. A strong, loyal workforce drives sustainable profitability.

Proof: Companies on Fortune's "100 Best Companies to Work For" list consistently outperform the market by 2 to 3 percent annually, showing that a people-first approach leads to superior financial performance over time.

6. **Stronger Company Culture and Reputation**

Organizations that lead with a "people over profits" approach build strong cultures, which enhances their brand reputation and attracts top talent and customers.

Proof: Glassdoor's "Best Places to Work" consistently shows that companies with strong people-first cultures attract and retain top employees, which contributes to these companies' long-term success.

What Will Your Legacy Be?

From time to time, I'll run into former team members—sometimes from decades ago—and I'm always struck by what they tell me. Many say that I was their favorite leader. Considering all the managers they would have had since our time together, I'm always flattered—and also curious. When I ask why, the answers are remarkably consistent:

"You got to know me as a person. You listened. You cared about me and my success. You helped me get what I wanted. No one has ever led me that way since."

At first, I would be surprised to hear something like that. Then I would reflect on how I learned to lead. It came naturally because I was drawn to the few leaders who had led me the same way—those who valued me as a person first, not just as a means to a goal. In contrast, many leaders I've encountered are solely focused on metrics: data, spreadsheets, and KPIs. It feels transactional, not transformational.

When I stepped into leadership, I fumbled around a bit and finally figured out that I wanted to do things differently. People first, accountability second. Once I had truly gotten to know my people, I could better support, challenge, and elevate them—and that became my driving priority. I didn't always get it right, and I continue to work on my leadership today. With that said, the legacy I strive for is simple but powerful:

To be a transformational and visionary leader who leads by example, inspires through action, uplifts those around me, and leaves every person, situation, and organization better than I found it—creating a lasting ripple of growth, excellence, and impact.

Hearing these reflections from former team members tells me that I've made meaningful progress—and inspires me to keep building that legacy every day.

Living with Legacy in Mind

In the book *Tuesdays with Morrie*, author Mitch Albom shares a profound insight from his beloved professor: "Once you learn how to die, you learn how to live."

At first glance, it feels paradoxical. But woven into those words is deep wisdom: When we fully accept that our time is limited, we begin to live—and lead—with greater purpose, urgency, and appreciation. We stop wasting moments. We start making them count.

Some leaders move through their careers aimlessly, focusing only on the day-to-day without ever defining the impact they hope to create. They lead by accident, not by design.

But lighthouse leaders lead with intention.

They have a vision—of the leader they want to become, the difference they want to make, and the ripple effects they want to leave behind. They understand that, though plans will evolve over time, having a guiding purpose is what matters most.

Leadership is one of the greatest opportunities to shape lives for the better. If you're going to invest your energy, why not build something truly lasting? Strive to be the leader who leaves people better, stronger, and more inspired than you found them. When you create an environment where others can grow, thrive, and dream bigger, you don't just change their lives—you amplify your legacy for generations.

There is no single formula for doing this. Your legacy will be uniquely yours. The important thing is this: positively impacting others and sparking ripple effects of growth, resilience, and achievement.

Consider the late Apple cofounder Steve Jobs. His name is synonymous with creativity and innovation—and for good reason. But Jobs was also famously demanding and, at times, difficult to work for. Yet his unwavering intensity pushed those around him to achieve breakthroughs they never thought possible. He didn't dilute his passion for excellence—he harnessed it to inspire greatness.

Now think of former US Secretary of State Madeleine Albright and Mother Teresa. Albright championed diplomacy and peace, fiercely defending human dignity on the world stage. Mother Teresa, though celebrated for her compassion, held uncompromising standards for service and sacrifice. Different missions, different contexts—yet both used their influence to lift people up and leave lasting legacies.

What connects leaders like these?

They stayed true to themselves and their purpose. They lived with vision and led with conviction. They never measured success by titles or accolades alone but by how deeply they elevated the lives around them. They didn't bend who they were to fit expectations—they stood firm in what they believed, and that made all the difference.

The same opportunity is in your hands.

Expert tip: first consider what kind of ripple effect you will choose to create.

Your Leadership Legacy Starts Now

Every action you take is a brushstroke on the canvas of your leadership legacy.

Every conversation, every decision, every time you choose people over profit, trust over fear, purpose over comfort—these are the moments that define you.

You don't have to wait for a title, a milestone, or a grand finale. Your legacy is being written today by how you lead right now.

Lead boldly. Lead with heart. And leave a mark that lifts others higher—and lasts for decades to come.

BOLD Takeaways

- **People first, always.** Lasting impact isn't built through profits or accolades; it's built through people. Focus on developing, uplifting, and empowering those you lead and your influence will ripple far beyond your time in the role.

- **Leadership is a long game.** Short-term wins at the expense of trust, morale, or sustainability may feel like progress, but true leadership legacy is measured by what continues to grow long after you're gone.

- **Your legacy is built daily.** Legacy isn't something you leave behind at the end; it's something you build with every conversation, every decision, and every moment of leadership. Be intentional. Be consistent.

- **Vision and purpose create ripples.** When you lead with clear vision and heartfelt purpose, you create a ripple effect that lifts others higher, sparking growth, innovation, and impact that carries forward for generations.

Chapter 12:
Leadership Legacy Exercise

Your leadership legacy isn't something that will be built someday. It's being built right now—through every action, every conversation, and every decision you make. This exercise will help you define your legacy with intention and bring it to life.

Step 1: Reflect on your legacy.
Answer these questions thoughtfully:
- What kind of leader do I aspire to be at my very best?
- What core values do I want my leadership to embody—even when no one is watching?
- How do I want the people I lead to feel because of my influence?
- What positive change do I hope my leadership sparks—in people, teams, and organizations?
- What lessons, behaviors, or beliefs do I want others to carry forward because of me?
- When challenges arise, what leadership traits do I want to be known for demonstrating?
- If my leadership could leave a ripple effect in the world, what would it be?
- In one sentence, how would I want my leadership story to be told?

Step 2: Choose your legacy words.
Review the list below. Circle five words that resonate most with the leader you aspire to be. You don't need to already be great at them. Just choose the ones that matter most to you.
Legacy words:
- Visionary
- Purpose-driven
- Integrity
- Authentic
- Empowering

- Impactful
- Inclusive
- Diverse
- Adaptable
- Innovative
- Relationship builder
- Community-focused
- Long-term thinker
- Resilient
- Courageous
- Emotionally intelligent
- Empathetic
- Sustainable
- Responsible
- Accountable

Step 3: Take inventory.
- Checkmark the qualities you believe you already embody.
- Circle the qualities you aspire to strengthen and grow into.

This gives you a snapshot of where you are today—and where you want to go next.

Step 4: Build your legacy plan.
For each aspirational quality, list one small action you can take to strengthen it. (Example: if "empowering" is aspirational, commit to asking your team for input before making key decisions.)
Ideas to help you grow:
- Research strategies and read books on the quality.
- Find role models who embody it well and learn from them.
- Ask your team or peers for feedback on how you show up today—and where you can grow.
- Leadership growth is intentional, not accidental. Brick by brick, you are building your legacy.

Step 5: Envision your legacy moment.

Imagine this: it's 10 or 20 years from now and someone you've led is giving a speech about you.

- What are they saying?
- What stories are they telling?
- What lessons do they say that they learned from you?
- Who is present to listen?

Write it down. This isn't about your organization—it's about YOU and the mark you want to leave on others.

Remember:

- The leadership legacy you create isn't about perfection; it's about impact.
- Every conversation, every act of care, every brave decision shapes it.
- It's not someday. It's today.

Daring Drive

From Vision to Victory

*"Take care of your days and your days will take care of your weeks.
Take care of your weeks and your weeks will take care of your
months. Take care of your months and your months will take care of
your years."*
—Old Proverb

Daring drive is the "D" in BOLD. It is the execution and action in leadership. It is where the rubber meets the road, where we take action and empower our teams to do the same. Most other leadership books stop before getting to this part, leaving the reader with inspiration and vision but without a plan for bringing them to reality.

The fact of the matter is that only effective execution will help us achieve BOLD leadership. Sure, a lot needs to happen before execution—innovation, ideation, strategy, more strategy—but at some point, we need to stop talking and start doing. We need to make some decisions and then take action. This is how we actually get to the part of doing what we need to do to realize our true potential and reach our vision.

Execution Matters—Lessons from the Field

Early in my career, I worked at a company where execution and accountability were nonnegotiable. Because I hadn't experienced anything different yet, I thought that was just how business worked everywhere. It wasn't until I moved on to a new organization that I realized how rare and valuable that culture truly was.

At first, the new company seemed promising, as they shared my passion for customer focus. But there was a critical flaw: they rarely moved beyond discussion into decisive action. Goals were set but rarely achieved—unless, of course, the goal was to set records for endless, circular meetings. That we excelled at!

Coming from a high-tech environment where decisions were made at lightning speed, the slow-motion pace of this new organization was maddening. I was used to driving progress, crossing things off my list, and seeing results. Here, my sense of urgency was met with pushback. I was told to slow down, socialize ideas more, gather more feedback, get more consensus. Meanwhile, real opportunities were passing us by.

Worse, instead of trusting the talented people already inside the organization—those closest to the customers and the challenges—we hired expensive consultants to tell us what we already knew. Analysis became our addiction. Paralysis became our culture.

It was one of the most frustrating seasons of my career but also an excellent learning experience. I often thought: if I had moved this slowly at my last company, I'd have been fired. But if I pushed too hard here, I'd probably be fired too. So now what?

That experience was a major eye-opener for me. I learned that execution is the critical missing link for many well-intentioned organizations. You can have the best culture, the best strategy, and the best intentions, but if you never get to the part where people are held accountable for results, you lose. Momentum stalls. Morale drops. Customers notice.

It's not enough to care deeply about leadership, engagement, and customer satisfaction. You have to act. You have to move. Otherwise, no matter how good your ideas are, they'll wither away in the land of "someday."

Sadly, too many organizations are still stuck there—circling endlessly, wondering why they aren't winning. I'll be the first to admit:

getting deep into the details isn't always my favorite part; it doesn't play to my strengths. Following processes, taking the linear steps, and grinding through the daily work can feel a lot like folding laundry: tedious and repetitive—but absolutely essential. Without putting in the reps, the vision stays a dream (and the laundry stays piled up).

The truth is that small consistent actions build big outcomes. But before we get to action, we must first decide how we want to achieve the vision. That's where systemizing comes in. There's real beauty in having a process—a way to automate progress, focus our energy, and move the needle every day.

And it all starts with setting the right goals.

Why Goals Are Your Growth Engine

Goals aren't just a leadership tool—they're also your engine for growth. Without clear goals, you're not leading. You're wandering. Goals give your team direction, focus, and fuel. They turn ambition into action and dreams into deliverables. Without them, it's impossible to know whether you're making real progress or just staying busy. Well-set goals break your vision into tangible steps, help you measure success, and create accountability across the team. They aren't just a nice-to-have—they're how you win.

I learned this firsthand with a sales group I coached recently. They had plenty of hustle and some impressive past success, but their strategy boiled down to one thing: close the next deal. No bigger plan, no measurable targets, no idea where they were actually trying to go. Success was happening in spite of their lack of clarity—not because of it.

When I stepped in, it was clear that they weren't just leaving opportunities on the table—they were leaving entire markets untapped. They needed a bigger vision—and the goals to make it real.

First, we zoomed out to see the full landscape: existing clients they could grow, prospects they hadn't touched, and new markets they could dominate. Then we broke it down, team by team and player by player. Everyone knew exactly what their target was and why it mattered.

The result? They stopped playing small. With clear goals tied to real strategy, they shifted from scrambling after random wins to systematically building momentum. They weren't just closing more deals—they were building a business.

Hope is not a strategy. Vague ambition won't get you there. Specific, bold, measurable goals will.

Setting the Right Goals

First things first: you can't hit a target you haven't set. When it comes to setting goals, there are three primary approaches.

Three Approaches to Goal Setting: Finding the Right Fit for Your Team

1. Top-Down Goal Setting

- Definition: Leadership sets goals and cascades them down to individuals or teams.
- When to use: Best when teams are newer and less experienced, or when organizational alignment is critical.
- Strengths: Clear direction, fast implementation.
- Pitfalls: Can feel disconnected or demotivating if employees have no input.

2. Bottom-Up Goal Setting

- Definition: Teams and individuals help set their own goals, which then roll up to inform organizational targets.
- When to use: Ideal for experienced, knowledgeable teams with strong market/client insight.
- Strengths: Builds buy-in, realistic targets, greater ownership.
- Pitfalls: Risk of "sandbagging" goals too low; can require more negotiation and time.

3. Hybrid Goal Setting

- Definition: Leadership sets broad targets or strategic priorities while teams collaborate to refine and own specific goals within that framework.
- When to use: Effective in most organizations, especially where you want balance between strategic alignment and team ownership.
- Strengths: Provides clarity from the top while empowering teams to tailor goals realistically.
- Pitfalls: Requires strong communication and trust; leaders must resist the urge to micromanage.

Remember, there's no one "perfect" model—the best approach often depends on your team's experience, the company's culture, and the complexity of the goals. But one thing is certain: when teams have clarity, connection, and ownership of their goals, execution becomes not just possible but powerful. The best leaders don't just pick one method—they flex based on what will best engage and unlock their team's potential.

Clarity

Being clear on both the goal itself and why it's important is a game-changer. When you're up front about what needs to be achieved and why, everyone gets the sense of direction they need. It's like having a map on a road trip: you know where you're headed and why that destination is where you want to go. Knowing what and why makes it easier for the team to determine if what they're doing each day is contributing to the bigger picture of the company's success. And they can't do that without both clarity of direction and the reason for that direction.

A perfect example of the importance of being clear not only on the goal but also why it's important is the Moviefone situation I discussed in chapter 11. To the team, the goal was to be on the phone more *because I had told them that I wanted them on the phone more*. The issue was that I wasn't clear on *why* they needed to be on the phone more: to talk to more potential customers in order to increase sales. If they had known this, they would have realized that being on the phone getting movie times was not actually getting them any closer to reaching our goals.

Think of it this way: If your team is making calls, punching in numbers, or handling tasks without knowing the impact, they easily lose motivation. They'll be thinking, *What is the point?* But when they understand that their work is a crucial piece of the puzzle that drives the company forward, it adds meaning to the daily grind. It's not just about hitting targets or wrapping up projects; it's about seeing the broader impact of their efforts.

Take a moment to explain to your team why the goal matters. Share how their contributions are essential to the company's mission. When everyone understands how their roles fit into the grand scheme, they're far more likely to be motivated and invested in the outcome. Plus, it builds a sense of teamwork and purpose. It's all about connecting the dots and making sure everyone sees the value in what they're doing.

Measurement

One of the most significant issues with goal setting is learning how to measure your goals. One way to ensure that they are practical is to use SMART goals. It's also important to have different types of measurements for various goals.

Qualitative goals focus on a project's or endeavor's subjective, nonnumerical aspects. They often relate to feelings, experiences, or perceptions.

Examples of qualitative goals include the following:
- Improving customer satisfaction
- Enhancing employee morale
- Strengthening community relationships
- Increasing brand awareness

Quantitative goals, on the other hand, tend to the SMART side, as they are specific, measurable, achievable, relevant, and time-bound. They involve numerical targets or benchmarks.

Examples of quantitative goals include the following:

- Increasing sales by 20 percent
- Reducing customer churn by 10 percent
- Hiring five new team members
- Completing a project within a specific timeframe

Instead of just looking at how someone's showing up (which, admittedly, is extremely important as well), we must be able to see the numbers, the hard facts. The more you can define a KPI, the better you can measure progress and adjust. Measurement is all about being objective.

KPIs can be tricky because they come in different flavors—some are short term, some are long term. Some are lagging behind, and some are leading ahead. And all are important. Take sales, for example. You're not just looking at end-of-quarter revenue; you're tracking daily activities that are lead indicators, such as the number of proposals sent out, calls made, contacts established, and meetings set up. By measuring these actions, you can better predict and influence your outcomes.

You want to ensure that your team has those leading indicators in place so they can see what's working in real time and adjust, as needed, in order to keep everything on track. This is different from looking back and seeing that you didn't hit your revenue goal in Q1. You can't change that now—that ship has sailed. These are lagging indicators, things that have already happened. But leading indicators? Those are where the gold is. They give you a heads-up on whether you're on track by measuring activities that are contributing to your goals.

Timeliness

Many find that, in order to achieve their goals effectively, they need to focus on smaller, more manageable steps. Rather than overwhelming ourselves with annual or quarterly targets, let's break down our objectives into monthly or even weekly goals.

This is where leading indicators become invaluable. They provide real-time insights into our progress and allow us to make necessary adjustments. Tracking daily activities is a simple but effective way to measure these indicators. For instance, suggest that team members maintain a daily log to monitor their progress on key tasks such as making calls or completing specific projects. At the end of each week, review your performance and identify areas for improvement. This will help you adjust your approach and stay on track toward your goals.

Individual accountability is essential, but leaders should also play a supportive role.

Expert tip: Help team members maximize their strengths and overcome challenges by providing coaching and guidance. If you notice a team member excelling in a particular area, explore ways to leverage their skills for greater impact.

Achievable

I'm a BIG FAN of stretch goals, but you also need to reach the realistic goals along the way. Sure, we want our teams to reach higher and strive for the most they can, but if they always fall short, their motivation and confidence take a huge hit. If you can't build the bridge to get there, then you need to readjust to be more realistic. The goals shouldn't be too easy, of course, but striking the right balance is essential. If you have historical data to look at, use it—past performance is a great predictor of the future. It gives us a solid foundation to build on and helps chart a path to where we want to go. Don't just pull numbers out of thin air; use accurate data to guide your goals. Looking at your past three years of performance is one of the best predictors of future success. Be grounded and use your information to make smart, achievable goals.

Here's a very simple example:

Setting a Revenue Goal Based on Historical Data

A company's revenue has been increasing steadily over the past three years. To set a realistic and ambitious goal for the coming year, let's analyze its growth rate and project future revenue.

Calculating the Average Growth Rate

Year 1 to Year 2: Growth Rate = ($150 million- $100 million)/$100 million = 50%

Year 2 to Year 3: Growth Rate = ($175 million- $150 million)/$150 million = 16.67%

Average Growth Rate: (50% + 16.67%)/2 ≈ 33.33%

Projecting Revenue for the Coming Year

Assuming a similar growth rate, we can project the revenue for the coming year:

Projected revenue [Year 3 revenue x (1 + AGR)] = $175 million x (1 + 33.33%) ≈ $233.33 million

Setting the Goal

Given the historical trend and projected revenue, a reasonable goal for the coming year could be $230 million. This goal would be ambitious but achievable based on the company's past performance and projected growth.

Additional Considerations

- Market conditions: Analyze the overall market trends and economic outlook to adjust the goal if necessary.
- Company strategy: Consider any new initiatives or changes in strategy that may impact revenue.
- Resource availability: Ensure that the company has the necessary resources (e.g., personnel, capital) to achieve the goal.

By setting a goal based on historical data and considering other factors, the company can create a realistic and challenging target that drives growth and performance.

Get Out of Their Way, But Stay Engaged

As leaders, our primary role after setting goals isn't to micromanage every move but rather to empower our teams by stepping back and supporting them where it counts. It's easy to fall into the trap of saying, "Here's what worked for me, so it should work for you," but this approach usually backfires. Each team member has unique strengths and challenges; what worked for you might not work for them.

Remember that your role as a leader is not to have all the answers. Instead, to be most effective in your role, you should have the best questions. Instead of dictating their path, focus on asking insightful, open-ended questions, encouraging them to reflect on their progress and solutions. For example:

- What's working well so far?
- What could be improved?
- What are the biggest obstacles you're facing right now?
- What have you done when faced with an obstacle such as this in the past?
- How can I help remove barriers or clear the way for you to make progress?
- What additional resources or support do you need to achieve your goal?

Your goal is to guide them in uncovering their own solutions. Doing so builds their confidence and problem-solving skills and enables them to take full ownership of their journey. You're there to support and challenge them—not to dictate how they should get things done. This is the essence of BOLD leadership: creating an environment where your team feels empowered to make decisions and chart their own course.

Of course, empowering your team doesn't mean turning a blind eye to progress or being an absentee leader when they need you most.

Regular check-ins are essential to ensure that things stay on track. These moments allow you to assess performance and course-correct if necessary without stifling your team's autonomy. If team members constantly come to you with problems, it's a signal that they may be too reliant on your involvement. Use it as an opportunity to step back and ask questions, encouraging them to think critically about their approach and find solutions independently.

Consider a situation early in my career when I was surprised by a smaller-than-expected commission check. After discussing it with my manager, we discovered the issue: though I had been selling many products, I hadn't been asking the right questions when selling products to customers. By simply processing their requests, I was missing critical insights into what they needed, leading to a high amount of returns. My manager helped me see that if I dug deeper and asked questions to truly understand their needs, I could better align the product with their expectations. As a result, my sales increased, returns decreased, my clients were much happier, and my pay reflected that growth.

The takeaway here is that thoughtful questioning can lead to breakthroughs. Ask your team questions that encourage reflection, clarity, and problem-solving, and you'll create an empowered environment where progress happens more naturally and barriers fall away.

The Importance of Measuring and Celebrating Progress

Celebrating small wins is the fuel that keeps a team moving forward. It's not just about the confetti moment; it's about showing people that what they do matters. But for celebration to mean something, everyone has to be rowing in the same direction.

I learned this firsthand when I introduced a revenue-based team goal to a group of people who had always operated individually. At first, they were skeptical—after all, they were used to running their own races. But as the team goal took hold, something shifted. Suddenly, wins weren't just personal—they were shared. When one person would land a new deal, the whole team would feel a sense of accomplishment, knowing that it moved everyone closer to success.

Alignment created momentum. Momentum created support. And support made every small victory sweeter. When people see how their individual work fits into the bigger picture, they stop competing with each other and start competing for each other. That's when the magic happens.

Here are some steps you can take:

1. **Set [the right] goals.** Make sure you set the right goals, backed by data. Define clear, achievable objectives by analyzing historical performance and relevant metrics to ensure that your goals are realistic and data driven.
2. **Monitor their progress.** Regularly track and review performance against these goals using KPIs to identify trends, address issues early, and keep everyone aligned with the targets.
3. **Get out of their way.** Empower your team by trusting them to handle their tasks independently while providing them with the freedom to innovate and make decisions without micromanagement.
4. **Offer support and guidance.** Be available to provide resources, feedback, and encouragement as needed, ensuring that your team has the tools and advice necessary to overcome challenges and achieve their objectives.
5. **Celebrate the small wins.** Acknowledge and reward incremental achievements along the way to maintain motivation, boost morale, and reinforce the value of progress toward the larger goal.

Remember: it's not just about setting targets but also about supporting your team and celebrating those small victories along the way. When you focus on these key elements, you'll turn your vision into real, impactful results. Goals help us find the right balance between vision and action—just what we need for daring drive!

BOLD Takeaways

- **Decisive action beats endless discussion.** Great ideas are worthless without execution. Stop circling and start moving—momentum is the bridge between vision and victory.

- **Goals turn dreams into deliverables.** BOLD leaders set clear, specific goals—and tie them to the bigger mission. Goals aren't just tasks; they're the milestones that turn ambition into real, measurable progress.

- **Empowerment unlocks ownership.** Set the vision, provide support, and then get out of the way. True leadership isn't about controlling every move; it's about building confident, capable teams that lead themselves.

- **Celebrate the climb, not just the summit.** Recognizing small wins along the way fuels energy, strengthens commitment, and reminds your team that every step forward matters. Progress *is* the path to greatness.

Chapter 13:
BOLD Goal Action Plan Exercise

Worksheet: From Vision to Victory
Execution is about doing the right things consistently. Use this simple worksheet to turn your vision into reality.

1. Big Goal:
What major outcome do you want to achieve? _____

2. Key Milestones: What 3–5 steps will get you there?

    1.

    2.

    3.

    4.

    5.

3. Daily/Weekly Actions: What consistent actions will drive your progress?
Actions:

-
-
-

4. Target Dates:
When will each milestone be completed? _____

5. Obstacles and Solutions: What challenges might arise—and how will you handle them?
Obstacle: _____ | Solution: _____
Obstacle: _____ | Solution: _____

6. Your *Why*:
What makes this goal important to you? _____

7. Accountability and Celebration:
How will you celebrate small wins? _____
Who will help hold you accountable? _____
Reminder: Goals give you direction. Action brings them to life.
Stay BOLD and move forward!

Drive What Matters

"If everything is a priority, nothing is a priority."
—Karen Martin

The pace of change we are currently experiencing in the business world is unprecedented. Most everyone is running fast and seriously over-scheduled. Are you too? Every new iteration of technology is intended to ease our burdens by automating tasks. With broad access to everything on the internet and now AI to help us access the data we want even faster, we should all be able to take a breath. Yet instead of using our newfound "free time" to take on important activities or to get some much-needed relaxation, we fill it with other tasks! Many of us have become addicted to being busy, feeling the need to fill all those little gaps that open up—with something, anything, to do right away.

Giving equal weight to emails, social media feeds, and news feeds means our brains never get a break. Our hectic lifestyles come from cultural and societal pressures that make us believe that being busy conveys a sense of importance and achievement. The pressure to succeed in today's competitive world can lead to overwork, and the access to social media and the "perfect" lives portrayed in those feeds can make leaders feel inadequate, like they should be doing more. Psychologically, we are rewarded for each completed task with a dopamine hit, which causes a positive feedback loop, making it feel great to be busy. For others, staying busy is a distraction from anxiety, depression, or other uncomfortable feelings. This can also feed people's need to have a sense of control and security. But is that notion real? Probably not.

The 25/5 Rule

There's a well-known story about Warren Buffett and his 25/5 rule—a powerful lesson in prioritization. It goes like this: Buffett, one of the most accomplished people of our time, would start with a blank sheet of paper and list his 25 top goals—big or small, personal or professional. Then he would circle the five most important ones. Those five would become his sole focus. As for the other 20? He wouldn't just set them aside—he would crumple the list up and throw it away.

This approach reflects Buffett's long-term investing philosophy as well: stay focused, avoid distractions, and be ruthless about your priorities.

But here's the real question: if it's that simple, why don't we all do it?

The answer isn't a lack of intelligence or effort. It's because real prioritization is hard. We fall into traps: trying to achieve everything at once, not wanting to disappoint others, reacting to every new crisis, fearing failure, and clinging to tasks we should delegate—plus one of the biggest culprits I see, what I call "bundling."

Bundling happens when organizations start with a few clear priorities and then sneak in more under each one. Suddenly, each "priority" has 10 sub-goals attached, and the original 5 have ballooned into 50. At that point, true focus is gone. You might technically complete all 50, but it will likely be with mediocrity, not mastery.

Buffett's insight was profound: Spreading ourselves too thin guarantees that we excel at nothing. Hard work alone doesn't create results—focused work does.

The truth is simple: If you want to go far, you have to go in fewer directions. Fewer goals. Deeper focus. Greater excellence.

Prioritization

In his book *Essentialism*, author Greg McKeown emphasizes the importance of identifying what truly matters for leaders.[xxi] If we try to impact too many areas at once, we can only make a shallow impression on each one. However, if we focus on a single area, our impact can be much more far-reaching.

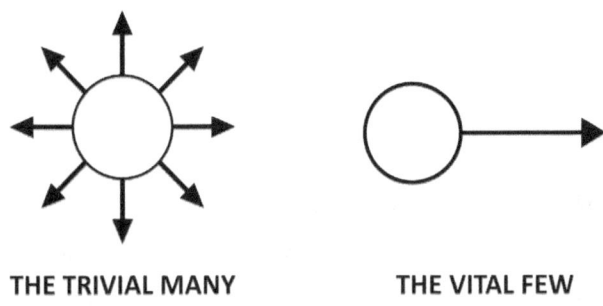

THE TRIVIAL MANY   **THE VITAL FEW**

Focus fuels impact

BOLD leaders know that they need to prioritize their actions properly to achieve what matters most. Their job is to use their heads more than their hands. Starting with your BOLD vision is the best way to ensure that you and your team are headed down the right path. Effectively, the BOLD vision will have a plan to achieve the desired results. This plan will have specific steps that need to be taken in order to realize the vision. Everything else is just noise—much of it should be ignored or deprioritized. BOLD leaders know that when things get hectic and start to feel out of control, it is time to step back, slow down, and think strategically. Take the time to prioritize what matters most and what deserves time, attention, and focus.

For many leaders, this may seem counterintuitive. That's because our ability to put our heads down and get work done is largely what got us promoted into leadership roles. Marshall Goldsmith wisely stated so himself in the title of his book, *What Got You Here Won't Get You There*. And this is very true for leaders. BOLD leaders understand the assignment and make time and space for strategic thinking, planning, and reflection. They must look up and outward, focusing on the big picture and thinking several steps ahead. Our environments are not static; market conditions change, supply-chain issues crop up, and clients continually ask for more; it's never-ending. If you are in the trenches, you won't be able to see any of it. Though you will remain busy, it won't be what matters most, and you will miss the opportunity to adjust. This busyness won't move you toward achieving your brilliant vision. Shifting from being busy to being strategic is crucial for effective leadership. Advancing in leadership requires us to be forward-thinking and leave day-to-day operations to our teams. It requires us to prioritize. Yet many leaders struggle to identify, let alone focus on, where they are needed most.

Prioritization Challenges

According to Gallup CliftonStrengths research, the number-one talent worldwide is being an Achiever™.[xxii] Achievers love to get things done every day and cross items off their lists. When they don't, they feel worthless. This drive is great for productivity but not always for focusing on the most important priorities for ourselves or for our teams. For example, if we know that we can only really excel at 3 priorities but we are expecting our teams to handle 10, how can we expect any of them to be done well? It's far better to focus on a few key areas and have our teams do the same. Though this is a struggle for many leaders (so much needs to get done!), when organizations hire us for leadership development or high performance, they rarely call on us to help their leaders prioritize. However, these issues frequently emerge as critical challenges once we dive deeper into our work with leaders and quickly get added to the agenda.

1. **Time Management**

   Time management is a challenge for leaders that often stems from a lack of prioritization. For example, many leaders need to delegate more. As discussed more fully in chapter 9, a leader should only be working in their Zone of Genius (the areas in which they are the best) and Zone of Excellence (the areas in which they are highly skilled). Everything in our Zone of Competence and Zone of Incompetence should be delegated or eliminated.

By delegating tasks appropriately, leaders can free up their time to focus on high-priority tasks that require their specific expertise and attention.

Another major hurdle with time management is procrastination. When leaders put off important and more complex tasks, they create a backlog that can overwhelm them later, leading to wasted time and missed opportunities. Effective time management means minimizing this misuse of time by cutting down on activities that don't contribute to the organization's goals and being more mindful of how our time is spent.

How can we manage our time better?

Developing strong time-management skills, prioritizing tasks effectively, delegating when necessary, and staying disciplined in avoiding procrastination are all keys to maximizing productivity and leading teams more effectively. Keeping what matters most at the top of the list will ensure that you are spending your time wisely and making progress.

2. **Focus and Concentration**
   Focus and concentration, though a large part of time management, are significant issues for most right now and emerge as their very own challenge. The never-ending barrage of distractions, such as the allure of scrolling through social media and constantly receiving email and text notifications, along with our thirst for instant gratification of responses, is contributing to significantly shortened attention spans, making it even harder for leaders to stay focused.[xxiii]

Additionally, this has become an even bigger issue with so many people working remotely and hybrid. Though it might seem like there would be fewer interruptions without coworkers stopping by for a chat or breaks to celebrate someone's birthday, and the commute time is nil, working remotely doesn't always mean fewer disruptions. Our homes have other distractions that arise: dogs barking, deliveries, interruptions from family and friends, noisy leaf blowers, unfinished home tasks—the list goes on. And don't get me started with all the beeps, dings, and notifications on our devices that constantly threaten our focus. (I shut mine off, by the way, and highly recommend you do too.) In fact, research shows that every time we get distracted, it can take up to 23 minutes to get back on track.[xxiv] That is a ton of waste!

We also see this daily need for more focus and concentration in social settings. People go out to dinner yet all are on their phones versus speaking with each other. For my daughter's 14th birthday, we hired a DJ, but her guests didn't even want to hear a full song! They preferred snippets of songs like they see on TikTok. Their attention spans have already adapted to short, quick bursts of content, and a whole song is too long. This demonstrates our challenge in maintaining focus in our increasingly fragmented, technology-driven world.

How can we spend more time being focused?

Block time on your calendar to do strategic work and focus on your top priorities. Start with 30 minutes if that is all you can spare and eventually work up to 2–3 hours. You will be amazed at how much high-quality work you can produce and the progress you will make.

3. Burnout

Another challenge we are seeing at a growing frequency today is burnout. We are social creatures, and because of that, we often say yes when we shouldn't. We do tasks others ask of us—feeling "honored" to have been asked—before completing our own essential work and then overwhelmed because we've taken on too much. We save imperative work for the end of the day when our energy is low, leading to subpar performance on the most crucial projects.

Imagine having an already packed schedule—work deadlines, family responsibilities, errands, and countless to-dos—when your daughter, partner, boss, or friend asks for "just one more thing." Naturally, you say, "Of course, I'll do it," even if it means stretching yourself to the brink.

This tendency is especially common among women in the workplace, who often put their own needs and well-being last to care for everyone else first. They're praised for being dependable, selfless, and always available—yet this can come at a steep cost. The constant "yes" can quietly erode their time, energy, and even their sense of self. Over time, this pattern can lead to exhaustion, burnout, and resentment—not to mention missed opportunities for growth and self-care. When you're too busy saying yes to everyone else, you have no time or energy left to say yes to yourself: your goals, your health, your own aspirations.

The truth is that setting healthy boundaries isn't selfish—it's a critical act of leadership for your own life. By learning to pause, check in with yourself, and say no, you make space to say yes to what matters most—and to show up fully for others *without losing yourself* in the process.

As leaders invariably act as the glue that holds everything together, what is the team supposed to do if we're sick, not working effectively, exhausted, or burned out? In this regard, and for our health, prioritizing self-care is crucial. Leaders must ensure that they're in good physical, mental, and emotional shape to support their teams. That's why it's important that we maintain our well-being and effectiveness by learning to say no and prioritize the essential tasks. The section on Oneness addresses this in detail.

These challenges impact everyone—and sometimes they impact me too. One of my top strengths is Input™, as I have a genuine curiosity and love learning about many different things and therefore have much to share. This trait allows me to engage in various topics and contribute diverse perspectives to discussions, which I love doing. Knowledge in a wide variety of areas can be incredibly advantageous, especially when brainstorming, problem-solving, and/or connecting the dots between seemingly unrelated concepts.

However, I've also found this strength to be a double-edged sword as my broad focus can sometimes pull me in too many directions at once, making it challenging to concentrate on a single task or project that requires deep focus and dedication. When precision and attention to detail are crucial, my tendency to scatter my attention can work against me. Balancing my innate curiosity with the need for focus is something I continually work on with various tools and resources. Setting timers to limit the amount of time I spend on research is one way I tame my thirst for knowledge and keep myself on track.

Leadership Is a Marathon, Not a Sprint

As I look back on my many years of leadership, I'm reminded of a personal experience that really makes the idea that leadership is more like a marathon than a sprint hit home. On our honeymoon, my husband and I drove down California's stunning Central Coast, traveling from Monterey to Cambria along Highway 1. The road was breathtaking with sweeping ocean views and towering cliffs, but behind the wheel, I gripped the steering wheel tightly. The Mustang convertible we'd rented was a thrill to drive, and I was eager to make good time, but as we rounded one tight curve after another, my husband, sensing my urgency, finally asked, "Why are you driving so fast?"

Without thinking, I answered, "We have to get there—this is taking a long time!"

He looked at me and said three simple words that stopped me in my tracks: "We are there."

I realized in that moment that he was right. The whole point of this journey was to experience the beauty of the California coast, to enjoy each moment. But my instinct to get from point A to point B as quickly as possible was turning a scenic drive into a rushed mission. In my type-A way of thinking, I was missing the most beautiful parts of the experience, reduced to a blur as we sped by.

Reflecting on my years in leadership, I realize that this habit of rushing forward doesn't apply only to road trips. Leadership, too, often feels like a relentless journey—a constant stream of responsibilities, challenges, and tasks. Remember those old dot-matrix printers, endlessly churning out paper in a noisy, continuous form? My to-do list often feels just like that: curves, venues, and tasks one after another with no clear stopping point.

That drive down Highway 1 taught me something important: sometimes, we're so focused on the destination that we miss the journey itself. In leadership, as in life, we need to slow down, take in the view, and realize that "we are there." Each step, each moment, is a part of the experience we don't want to rush past. And when we have this increased awareness of the moment, we become more self-aware.

We often delude ourselves into thinking that the pace will slow down after the next deadline or that we can "power through" just one more project. But the reality is that leadership is a continuous journey. There will always be another challenge, another goal, and another demand on our time. The key to thriving as a leader is learning how to pace yourself, focus on what is most important, and build the resilience needed to navigate the ups and downs of the journey. By prioritizing our own well-being, we can lead more effectively, inspire others to do the same, and create environments where both leaders and teams can thrive for the long haul.

This is where prioritization comes in. We must metaphorically tear apart that to-do list at some point and say, "Enough!" If you think you can power through it all, remember: there's always another box of tasks waiting. The key is learning to pause, prioritize, and recognize when to step back.

Prioritization Tools

Over the years, working with leaders and teams, I've gathered and refined a set of powerful prioritization tools. Here are a few of my favorites:

The Priority Matrix

The Priority Matrix is a tool for managing tasks. It categorizes them into four quadrants: Manage, Focus, Avoid, and Limit. The goal for leaders is to spend most of our time in the Focus quadrant, which involves critical thinking and important—but not urgent—tasks, those tasks that aren't a fire but are essential for the long-term success of the organization. Typically, we spend too much time on urgent tasks because we neglect the important ones until they become urgent. In one company I worked with, the entire leadership team actually thrived in this type of firefighting. They enjoyed the adrenaline rush of solving urgent problems quickly. But in the process, they made everyone exhausted and wasted resources.

The Manage quadrant involves pressing problems that should be delegated, similar to those tasks in your Zone of Competence and Zone of Incompetence. A great example of this is when someone brings you a problem. Instead of providing a solution, like many leaders do, ask questions to help them figure out the solution and be able to solve it on their own next time. The Avoid quadrant consists of interruptions and busy work, while Limit contains trivial and wasteful tasks. For Avoid, this is where you want to politely defer requests for help, suggesting alternative times that are better for you. For tasks in the Limit quadrant, such as checking social media or playing Wordle, you want to set clear boundaries to ensure that you're not wasting valuable time on trivial activities. This includes being restricted to non-peak energy times.

Managing Energy

The idea of focusing on energy comes from the book *The Productivity Project* by Chris Bailey. We all have times during the day when our energy levels increase and decrease. When we are on the upswing, we feel better, have clearer thinking, and are more focused. When our energy is low, we feel tired and have difficulty concentrating on things. Don't ignore these shifts in energy! Though they are different for everyone, understanding them is vital for prioritization. Effectiveness increases when our energy levels are high, whereas procrastination most often strikes when our energy is low.

Focus on when you have the most energy. *Is your optimal time for peak performance in the morning, afternoon, or evening?* Whichever it is, block off these high-energy periods for focused work.

If you're unsure, try keeping an energy log for a week. Track every-thing you do, noting when you feel most and least energetic. This exer-cise can reveal your energy peaks and valleys and also any surprising gaps in your schedule, revealing that you might have more free time than you realize. For instance, you might discover that your energy is consistently higher in the mornings throughout the week, suggesting that this is your ideal time for tackling essential tasks.

Using an energy log helps you identify these patterns and high-lights the space in your workday for both productive and enjoyable activities. By understanding your energy flow, you can better manage your time, leading to more-efficient workdays and a greater sense of accomplishment. Plus, it's a fun way to learn about your work habits and improve your productivity. Many of the leaders we work with who do this find availability in their schedules that can be more effectively utilized.

Incorporating moments of rest into your routine can also make a big difference. Simple activities such as daydreaming, taking a walk, or changing your scenery can stimulate creativity and offer a fresh per-spective. Leaving the confines of your office or home to enjoy nature or simply a different environment can help clear your mind and inspire new ideas, making it far easier to come back focused and ready to tackle what is most important.

Get Moving

With regard to avoiding burnout and increasing our overall health, a study by Columbia University and NPR looked at the difference between those who sit way too much during the day (most of us) and those who don't.[xxv] The question to be answered was, *What is the dif-ference with those who don't sit too much?* For six weeks, the study subjects committed to moving every 30 minutes. They would work at their desk for 25 minutes and then take 5 minutes to walk around or do some activity. Admittedly—and perhaps surprisingly—doing so was rather difficult. But when they did, their cholesterol and blood pressure decreased, along with their fatigue. At the same time, their focus and positive emotions increased. The number of breaks they took directly correlated to better results. And though this may seem counterintuitive to improve productivity, that's precisely what it did.

Working with our clients, especially during our one-on-one sessions, I often suggest a "walk and talk" meeting instead of the usual Zoom call. We'll each grab our phone and go for a walk alone—and we get everything done while moving. My clients, who are as tired of Zoom as we all are, absolutely love it! This works just as well in an office setting. Walking meetings provide a refreshing change of pace. They allow for more open and dynamic conversations, free from the constraints of a traditional office setting. The natural environment can stimulate creativity and reduce stress, making it easier for us to think clearly and share our thoughts openly. The physical activity of walking helps to boost energy levels and improve overall well-being and can enhance focus and engagement. The movement itself keeps us more alert and attentive, leading to more productive discussions.

Rule of Three

This is an effective tool that each of us can use every day simply by asking ourselves, *What are the three things that, if I accomplish them by the end of the day, will make me feel productive?* These should be three activities or tasks in your Focus quadrant that are important. Then, similar to the Warren Buffet 25/5 example, focus only on those three things. This takes practice and a lot of discipline, but it becomes much easier to implement daily when you see the difference it makes in your productivity.

Time Blocking

As previously discussed, burnout creeps in when we try to do everything but accomplish nothing, leaving us feeling like a failure or that we can never catch up. To combat this, execute tasks in manageable time chunks, such as 30–60 minutes. Often, once you're in the zone, you'll find that you'll likely keep going. It's best to avoid distractions and stay focused during these time blocks in order to maximize productivity.

You can also block out time based on specific activities: working on your business, dealing with clients, strategizing, catching up on tasks. Doing so is beneficial to our psyches because when we constantly switch between tasks, it is hard on the brain. Remember, it takes about 20 minutes to get back on track with whatever you were initially doing before you switched to focusing on something else. That time adds up throughout the day.

Darren Hardy's program *Insane Productivity* offers a 12-module course on productivity that emphasizes making time to think and do focused work every day.[xxvi] Hardy advocates working on something intensely for 90 minutes per day—no distractions, no breaks.[xxvii] I know that doing so sounds impossible to most. But what if you started smaller? Even dedicating just 30 minutes a day to uninterrupted, focused work—no email, no phone, no distractions—can yield significant benefits. The more we focus on the vital work, the better we will be.

Reflection

In today's culture, we often feel pressure to fill every moment with noise—conversation, music, distractions—anything to avoid the discomfort of silence. Yet it's in those quiet spaces that real clarity emerges. Silence gives us the rare chance to step back, reflect, and reconnect with what truly matters: How are we doing? Where are we excelling? Where do we need to grow? How could we do things better?

Without moments of stillness, true reflection is impossible.

Expert tip: Shut off the video. Turn off the music. Step outside. Go for a walk. Disconnect. And think.

You'll be amazed at how stepping away from the noise and immersing yourself in a peaceful environment sparks fresh ideas, deeper insights, and renewed focus. And the beauty of it? You don't need a plane ticket or a retreat—you can create that space for yourself, anytime, anywhere.

In a world obsessed with doing more, BOLD leaders know that the real power lies in doing less—with excellence. True prioritization isn't just about managing a list; it's about choosing a direction and giving it everything you have. When we focus on what matters most, we amplify our impact, energize our teams, and avoid the burnout that comes from trying to do it all. Leadership isn't about staying busy; it's about staying intentional. Focus fuels progress. Prioritization creates power. By choosing fewer, we achieve greater.

BOLD Takeaways

- **Focus is a leadership superpower.** You can't make an extraordinary impact if you're spread too thin. BOLD leaders prioritize ruthlessly and execute relentlessly.

- **Prioritization requires discipline.** Saying yes to the vital few means courageously saying no to the trivial many.

- **Energy management fuels execution.** Align your priorities with your highest-energy times—and protect that time fiercely.

- **Success is built through strategic simplicity.** Big wins aren't achieved through busyness; they come from bold focus, deep work, and clear direction.

Chapter 14:
Prioritize Like a BOLD Leader Exercise

Worksheet: Spend Time on What Matters Most

Execution without focus leads to burnout. Use the Priority Matrix below to prioritize your efforts. This exercise helps you spend more time where it matters most: on high-impact activities that move your vision forward.

Step 1: List your current tasks.

Write down all the tasks, projects, and responsibilities currently on your plate:

_____

_____

_____

Step 2: Sort tasks into the Matrix.

Use the Priority Matrix below to place each task into the correct quadrant.

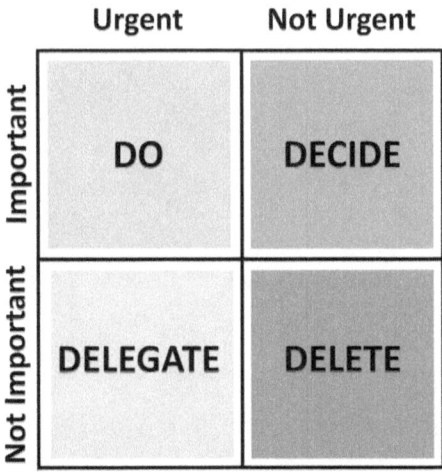

PRIORITY MATRIX

	Urgent	Not Urgent
Important	DO	DECIDE
Not Important	DELEGATE	DELETE

Master your time by mastering your choices—urgent isn't always important.

Step 3: Plan your next actions.
- **Focus quadrant:** Spend the majority of your time here. Block dedicated time for these activities on your calendar.
- **Manage quadrant:** Handle or delegate quickly. Prevent these tasks from becoming fires.
- **Avoid quadrant:** Minimize interruptions. Set boundaries and politely defer wherever possible.
- **Limit quadrant:** Eliminate or restrict these activities. These are time-wasters!

Reflection Questions:
- What surprised me about how my tasks were distributed?
- What will I do differently this week to stay in my Focus quadrant?
- What's one task I will eliminate or say no to this week?

Prioritization is a daily discipline. Start and end your day by checking your Priority Matrix.
Let's go!

Multiply Your Impact

*"The essential question is not 'How busy are you?' but
'What are you busy at?'"*
—Oprah Winfrey

I once heard a leadership expert say, "Your calendar tells me everything I need to know about what you value."

And it stopped me cold in my tracks.

When I looked at my calendar, it was packed—but not with what mattered most to me. It was overflowing with responsibilities tied to what others wanted from me, not to what I truly valued. People pleasing, "shoulds," and endless obligations filled my days, while the things I cared about most were squeezed into the margins—if there was any time left at all.

The hard truth? My calendar was full—really full—and the important things kept getting pushed down the road to a "someday" that never seemed to come. Sound familiar?

It wasn't until I did a values exercise that everything became clear to me: it was time for a change. The exercise I used came from *The Leadership Challenge* by James Kouzes and Barry Posner—a well-known framework that helps leaders define what they truly stand for. A values exercise like this is a simple but powerful reflection where you take time to identify and name the core principles that matter most to you—things such as family, integrity, health, creativity, freedom, or making a difference.

When I finally put my core values down on paper, I could see in black and white what really mattered—and what didn't. That clarity gave me the courage to make new choices. It helped me align how I spent my time with what I said was important instead of constantly reacting to everyone else's demands. It became a filter for my decisions, big and small, so I could start living—and working—on purpose, not on autopilot.

We often think we're clear on our priorities, but until we see them right in front of us, it's easy to drift. Doing a values exercise like the one from *The Leadership Challenge* grounds you in what matters most—so you can lead and live every day with intention.

What does this have to do with working smarter? Everything.

Taking a step back made me realize that I wasn't just overscheduled; I was working inefficiently. I needed to stop letting urgency crowd out importance. I needed to work smarter, and that started with aligning my actions with my values.

In the previous chapter, we discussed prioritization as a key to BOLD leadership. But prioritization alone isn't enough. Working smarter means choosing what matters most and being fiercely intentional about how you spend your time. It's about focusing your energy on what drives your goals forward, not just what screams the loudest for your attention.

Many Routes to Get to One Destination

At a technology company where analytical and financial skills were highly prized, I coached a client who faced a familiar trap: confusing what was valued with what was necessary.

He had an MBA, sharp business instincts, and a strong track record. Yet his boss insisted that he master detailed financial analysis in order to advance his career, because that was the approach that he had taken himself. The supervisor urged him to take finance classes, believing that developing such skills were the key to success.

The boss was change wrong to short-sighted. What my client needed wasn't another certification or spreadsheet. He needed a smarter strategy. Instead of trying to become a finance expert, he learned to prepare differently. Before big meetings, he partnered with his finance department to sharpen his readiness. He anticipated questions, validated answers, and stayed focused on his strengths—leading, influencing, and moving the business forward. He didn't need to do everything to win. He needed to do the right things with excellence.

Feedback is useful, but it's not gospel. Leaders must have the courage to filter advice through the lens of their own strengths and strategy. Working smarter means knowing where to double down—and where to delegate, collaborate, and/or prepare differently. The same mindset applies when leading others.

We worked with another leader who was good at asking questions to guide his team but struggled with accountability. He could help them solve the first problem but was unable to build momentum beyond it. When he came to me for advice, I didn't hand him a checklist. I asked him one simple question: "What would you do if you were in their shoes?"

As he worked through it, the answer revealed itself. That was the shift he needed to coach his people: to develop thinkers, not order-takers.

Working smarter isn't about your personal output. It's about creating a team that thinks smarter, acts faster, and delivers bigger outcomes—without depending on you for every next move. BOLD leaders don't just work smarter for themselves. They teach their teams to work smarter too—and that's how real success scales.

The Role of Mindset

Mindset isn't just important; it's everything when it comes to working smarter and achieving real success. For many leaders, busyness becomes a badge of honor. Their worth feels tied to how packed their calendars are. But true productivity isn't about doing more; it's about doing what matters most. Working smarter requires continuous reflection:

- Am I spending my time on the right things?
- Am I willing to pivot when necessary to stay aligned with my bigger goals?

One of my former leaders once shared a simple but powerful exercise that stuck with me. Just ask yourself, "Am I doing the most important thing right now?"

If yes, keep going. If not, stop and shift your focus to what truly matters.

This ties directly into what Dr. Carol S. Dweck highlights in her groundbreaking book *Mindset*.[xxviii] Dweck's research shows that success isn't just about intelligence or talent; it's about adopting a growth mindset.[xxix] People with a growth mindset believe that they can develop their abilities through effort, learning, and perseverance. They aren't paralyzed by setbacks or stay busy for busyness's sake—they learn, adapt, and improve.

A growth mindset isn't about doing more. It's about getting better—and smarter—over time.

It encourages leaders to view every action as a chance to learn and prioritize what will move them forward rather than just staying busy to feel accomplished.

> *"10x is not about working harder. It's about working differently, on the right things."*
> —Dan Sullivan & Dr. Benjamin Hardy

Dan Sullivan and Dr. Benjamin Hardy expand this idea even further in *10x Is Easier Than 2x*. They argue that small, incremental improvements (what they call "2x thinking") often trap us in old ways of working. True breakthroughs—"10x thinking"—require bold shifts, focusing only on the few activities that truly multiply impact.

Here's the counterintuitive truth: it's easier—and more energizing—to aim for 10x growth than to grind your way to a 2x improvement.

When you let go of the need to "do it all," you free yourself to think bigger, move faster, and lead smarter. You amplify your results without amplifying your workload. That's smart. That's BOLD leadership.

Empowering Your Team: The Crossroads of Delegation and the Zone of Genius

The true power of working smarter is recognizing that we don't have to do it all. By adopting an exponential mindset, focusing on abundance, and strategically leveraging the strengths of others, we can achieve far more while doing less—and with far less stress along the way. Having a clear understanding of both what you should do and what you should empower others to do is crucial.

I once worked with an incredibly effective boss who excelled at tactical execution. He was often right there with us, rolling up his sleeves and getting things done, which we appreciated. However, what we really needed from him was a broader, strategic perspective. We would occasionally remind him to "get back in the helicopter," as his ability to see the bigger picture from above was essential for guiding us forward. His hands-on involvement, though well intentioned, was our responsibility to manage.

What we needed most from him was to focus on setting the vision and goals, leaving us to determine the best ways to achieve them. Leadership is not just about working hard; it's about working smart—and knowing when to step back and provide strategic direction.

Outsourcing allows us to reclaim valuable time and focus on what we do best. Consider a common decision we all face: should we spend an hour picking something up or pay $25 to have it delivered? If your time is worth more than $25 an hour, the smarter choice is clear: outsourcing. Yet many of us fall into the trap of being penny-wise and pound-foolish. We try to save a small amount of money but end up depleting time that could be spent on more meaningful work.

This mindset can feel efficient—cutting small costs here and there—while we miss opportunities to make better, higher-impact decisions. We focus on minor details at the expense of the bigger picture.

Here's a simple way to calculate the value of your time:
- Annual salary: $150,000
- Hours worked per week: 50

- Annual working hours: 50 hours/week × 52 weeks = 2,600 hours/year
- Hourly rate: $150,000 ÷ 2,600 = $57.69 per hour

If your time is worth $60 an hour, does it make sense to spend it on administrative tasks you could delegate for half that cost? The real investment is focusing your time and energy on the high-value activities that create the greatest return. Outsourcing nonessential tasks isn't just a cost-saving tactic; it's a growth strategy.

For leaders earning at higher salary ranges, the math becomes even more compelling: the more valuable your time, the more critical it is to delegate lower-impact work and protect your focus for what matters most. Elevating your impact starts with elevating how you spend your time.

Working smarter by focusing on the high-impact activities that align with your strengths is leveraging your Zone of Genius that we talked about in the last chapter—the areas where you excel and are most effective—rather than getting bogged down in tasks that drain your energy or aren't the best use of your time. This is where the principle of *Who Not How: The Formula to Achieve Bigger Goals Through Accelerating Teamwork*, another concept and book by Dan Sullivan and Dr. Benjamin Hardy, comes into play.[xxx] Instead of asking, "How can I do this?" we should be asking, "Who can do this for me?"

Leaders often feel the need to do everything themselves—especially the tasks they personally dislike—assuming that others will dislike doing them too. But that's a major misconception. In reality, there are people whose strengths and passions align perfectly with the work we find draining. By delegating, we not only reclaim our own time but also create opportunities for others to thrive in their own unique Zone of Genius.

Let me share a lesson from one of my least proud leadership moments. Early in my career, when I first started working with an assistant, I struggled with delegation. Every time I handed off a task, I would apologize: "I'm so sorry to give you this—it's awful!" I thought I was being empathetic. Instead, I was unintentionally sending a damaging message—that the work was low value, unpleasant, and something no one would want to do. I was undercutting both the task and her confidence.

It wasn't until I reflected, with the help of the CliftonStrengths assessment, that I saw the problem clearly. I realized that the tasks I dreaded were often right in her Zone of Genius—and she actually enjoyed them. What drains one person can energize another.

Once I understood that, I changed my approach completely. I stopped apologizing and started celebrating strengths: "You are amazing at this—I'd love for you to take it on." The difference was immediate. Team members lit up, taking pride in the work and feeling valued for their unique abilities. Delegating became a win-win: the right people doing the right work, with energy and excellence.

The way we frame delegation matters. When we delegate with confidence and respect, we empower others—and ourselves—to work smarter, not harder.

Lead by Letting Go

One of the greatest ways leaders can drive performance—and build a strong, self-sufficient team—is by empowering others to step up. Empowerment isn't about stepping away from responsibility; it's about creating the space for your team to grow, take ownership, and thrive. True empowerment starts with clarity. When you delegate a task or assign a project, be crystal clear about the desired outcome, timing, and standards for success. Ambiguity kills momentum. When people know exactly where they're headed, they can move with confidence and creativity. Think of yourself as setting the destination and trusting your team to choose the best route.

Setting expectations early and often is another essential ingredient. Don't wait until something goes off course to clarify what good looks like. Paint a vivid picture of success from the beginning: what needs to happen, by when, and why it matters. High standards, paired with clear guidance, elevate performance and ensure that everyone knows what they're working toward. Have them repeat back to you in detail their understanding of the assignment so you have a chance to ensure understanding and make any needed corrections before work gets too far down the road.

Early in my career, a leader asked me to create a detailed business plan for the division I was leading. I had never written one before, but I was determined to deliver something exceptional. I spent months researching, collaborating with senior executives, and building a robust, strategic plan. I poured everything I had into it.

When I proudly handed it to my boss, expecting appreciation, he looked at it with confusion and asked, "What is this?" He didn't look pleased. He then exasperatedly explained that he didn't want a full business plan at all—he just needed a simple project timeline, something like a construction schedule, for building a house.

I was crushed. Not only had I invested countless hours on the wrong deliverable, but the sting didn't end there. He pulled out my business plan during meetings with my peers—not to praise the effort but to use it as an example of "what not to do." Each time, the humiliation cut deeper.

Looking back, this painful moment taught me two powerful leadership lessons:

1. Leaders must set crystal-clear expectations from the start. Without them, even the most dedicated team members can end up running hard in the wrong direction.
2. If expectations are unclear, it's your responsibility to keep asking questions until they are. Don't assume. Push for clarity. In leadership—as in life—misaligned assumptions are expensive.

Empowering leadership isn't about handing out assignments and walking away; it's about setting clear expectations, offering early course corrections, and treating every effort—successful or not—with respect. Great leaders guide; they never humiliate. Once expectations are set, shift your focus to regular, supportive check-ins, not micromanagement. Checking in is about partnering for success, not policing progress. Create a rhythm of short, meaningful conversations that uncover obstacles, celebrate wins, and offer support. Trust grows when your team knows that you care about their success, not just the work. Stay high level and outcome focused and resist the temptation to dive into the weeds. True empowerment thrives when leaders elevate instead of control.

As you look at your own workload, ask yourself this powerful question: "What am I doing today that someone else could take over tomorrow?" If your plate is overflowing, you're not empowering; you're hoarding. Identify tasks outside your Zone of Genius that are in someone else's and ripe for delegation. Free yourself to focus on the few things that create the most value—and allow others to rise by giving them ownership.

One of the best ways to do this is through stretch assignments. Give your team members opportunities to lead projects, solve new problems, and build skills that stretch them just beyond their current comfort zone. Stretch assignments signal that you believe in someone's potential. They light a fire of growth and build the next generation of leaders. Your role is to support and guide, not to rescue. Let them struggle a bit, because real confidence is built through effort, not ease.

Empowering your team isn't a soft skill; it's a strategic skill. When you lead by letting go, you multiply the impact of your leadership. You create more capable, confident people who own their results—and who, in turn, will help you achieve a vision far bigger than what you could ever accomplish alone.

Get Tactical in Order to Be Strategic

Take Bridget, for example. When she was promoted from senior director to VP of her company, everything changed—fast. Suddenly, she wasn't just responsible for what was happening now; she was responsible for what needed to happen three years from now. Yet her calendar didn't get the memo. It was jammed with day-to-day meetings, leaving her no space to step into the future-focused thinking her new role demanded.

At first, she tried squeezing in strategic time at night, but exhaustion always won. Sound familiar?

The turning point came when we got intentional. Bridget started fiercely protecting blocks of time on her calendar—time dedicated purely to thinking, planning, and imagining what's next. Within a few months, everything shifted. She walked into leadership meetings with a whole new presence—able to connect dots, see opportunities ahead, and shape conversations from a strategic point of view. Her impact skyrocketed. And it all started with one powerful move: creating space to think like the leader she was meant to be.

Expert tip: remember that working smarter doesn't happen by accident—it happens by design.

It's easy to fall into the trap of believing that our old habits will carry us to new heights. They won't. Success at the next level isn't about doing more of what made you successful in the past. It's about thinking differently, leading differently, and focusing relentlessly on what matters most.

Working smarter means managing more than tasks. It's managing your energy, your focus, and your vision. It's being intentional with every hour you spend. It's prioritizing high-impact activities, eliminating the distractions, and refusing to confuse busyness with progress.

And it's a practice, not a project. Smart leadership builds habits that sustain high performance over the long haul. It creates systems that protect time for strategy, innovation, and growth—not just today's urgent demands. It values quality over quantity, momentum over motion, and meaning over checking boxes.

Working smarter is how you move from reacting to shaping. From executing to leading. From staying busy to building a legacy. Make the shift. Protect your brilliance. Focus where it matters.

Working smarter isn't just about doing more in less time. It's about doing the right things with energy, clarity, and purpose. True progress happens when we align our actions with what matters most, empower others to step into their strengths, and protect our focus for the highest-value work. It's a mindset shift from busyness to BOLDness, from checking boxes to creating impact. BOLD leaders aren't just efficient—they're intentional, strategic, and committed to multiplying their results by working differently, not harder. When we prioritize our Zone of Genius, elevate our teams, and carve out space for strategic thinking, we build legacies, not just to-do lists.

BOLD Takeaways

- **You don't scale by doing more—you scale by doing the right things with focus, energy, and intention.** BOLD leaders resist the trap of busyness and choose actions that drive their vision forward.

- **Delegation and empowerment aren't a loss of control—they multiply impact.** When you empower others to operate in their Zone of Genius, everyone wins—and your leadership expands.

- **Strategic time isn't a luxury—it's a necessity.** Protecting space to think, plan, and lead is how leaders shift from managing to-day to shaping tomorrow.

- **The smartest work starts with a mindset shift.** True growth and smarter leadership come from embracing abundance, thinking 10x bigger, and focusing where it matters most—not reacting to everything that demands your attention.

Chapter 15:
Multiply Your Impact Journal Prompts

1. Where is my calendar aligned with what I value most, and where is it not?
Where am I spending time out of obligation rather than intention?

2. When am I being BOLD versus just busy with my time?
Which activities are high impact, and which are just noise?

3. What's one task I'm doing that someone else could own?
Whom could I give it to so that it would help them develop and grow?

4. How often am I operating in my Zone of Genius?
What energizes and drains me? What should I do more of and delegate?

5. What is the *why* behind what I'm doing right now?
What's the deeper purpose?

6. Where could I create more space to think strategically each week?
Where can I protect more time for future-focused leadership?

7. What feedback have I received that I need to filter through my own lens?
Where am I following someone else's path instead of forging my own?

8. Where are additional opportunities to empower others with stretch assignments?
Who on my team is ready to take on more—and grow as a result?

9. What's one small shift I can make to work 10x smarter this month?
Where can I go bigger by doing less?

10. What legacy am I building with how I lead my time and use my energy?
What do I want to be known for? What needs to change for me to get there?

--- **Chapter 16** ---

Drive Through the Difficult

"It's not that I'm so smart; it's just that I stay with problems longer."
—Albert Einstein

The bigger your vision, the bigger the obstacles. But with daring drive, those obstacles become stepping stones—fuel for the boldest break-throughs. For BOLD leaders, it is not a matter of if but when we are going to face obstacles and failure. They come in many forms and from many directions, and they come up often. Maybe it's an internal challenge—something impacting a certain department, the team, or a policy/procedure. Or maybe it's an external challenge with a spe-cific client, the industry, or some other socioeconomic force. There are simply always going to be problems that need our attention and that need it quickly.

Throughout this book, we've talked about how leaders often deal with some of these issues; specifically, that we often find ourselves trapped in a cycle of putting out fires—constantly addressing immedi-ate issues that demand attention. No sooner does one get solved than another pops up (think: Whac-a-Mole!). And though it's important to tackle these problems before they escalate, it's equally important to recognize that these issues are often signs of deeper, underlying chal-lenges within the organization.

Failure Is an Option

Nvidia CEO Jensen Huang shared an insightful observation in an interview when asked what important advice he would share with leaders who want to build a business: "If you want to be successful, I encourage you to grow a tolerance for failure."[xxxi] "If you fail often enough, you actually might become a failure—and that's different than being successful," he explained. "So the question is, *How do you teach someone how to fail, but fail quickly?* And to change courses as soon as you know it's a dead end?"[xxxii]

The answer, according to Huang, is something called intellectual honesty. The approach is straightforward: "We assess on a continuous basis whether something makes sense or not. And if it's the wrong decision, let's change our mind."[xxxiii]

He went on to contend that to create a company capable of inventing "amazing things that solve problems for the world that it sometimes didn't even know it had," building a tolerance for risk-taking is crucial. At the same time, it's also essential to "teach people how to fail but fail quickly and inexpensively."[xxxiv]

According to Huang, this mindset is vital because innovation is predicated on experimentation, which necessitates exploration, and exploration may lead to failure.

"Unless you have a tolerance for failure, you will never experiment, and if you don't ever experiment, you will never innovate. If you don't innovate, you don't succeed," he concluded.[xxxv]

Assessing the Real Issue

When leaders become so consumed with solving the crises at hand, they generally don't take the time to step back and figure out the root causes behind them. They feel as if they don't have a choice. They have to take care of whatever is right in front of them. Many public companies are especially susceptible to this with their short-term obsessions with quarterly results. If you look in technology, patches are delivered to solve small problems versus system challenges being addressed. In healthcare, the focus is on resolving patient-care issues without addressing the big problems with staffing and turnover. In manufacturing, equipment breakdowns might cause repeated failures if regular maintenance isn't handled properly. The list goes on and on.

Don't even get me started with pharma, where the focus on symptoms rather than root causes is even more pronounced. Drug development tends to focus on symptom management versus shifting business models toward value-based care where the incentives come from long-term patient outcomes rather than short-term symptom management. My parents, in their early 80s, have multiple medications they take each day, which actually has a term assigned to it: "polypharmacy." The challenges with taking this many medications include increased risk of negative drug interactions, adverse drug reactions, nonadherence and errors, costs, cognitive and physical challenges, and, well—there are a lot more issues. I thank my lucky stars for my sister and her medical training, as she helps them manage their medications. Doctors, pharmacies, and other caregivers are fragmented and lack coordination, so patients and families are required to take this burden on themselves.

When we take a reactive approach to anything, it leads to a never-ending cycle of firefighting, where too much time and energy is spent on treating surface-level problems rather than addressing the core issues that initially ignited and continue to feed the flames.

Most leaders are squeezed for time and have too many priorities, so they end up not asking enough questions to truly understand what the real problem is. If they did, they would understand that the issues that surface are often merely the symptoms of something else. And though those symptoms also need to be resolved, when leaders effectively address the root problems, those symptoms will go away for good. Bye-bye firefighting (or at least a lot of it)!

When I was up for a promotion—a newly created role focused on building a post-sales customer-resolution team—I sat down with the CEO for the final interview. Toward the end of our conversation, he said something I'll never forget: "I don't want you to get good at solving customer issues. I want you to be great at preventing them from happening in the first place."

At the time, I thought I understood what he meant. But over the years, I've realized that it was one of the most important lessons of leadership.

BOLD leaders don't just react faster—they think deeper.

They have the discipline to pause, assess, and get curious. Instead of asking, "How do we fix this problem right now?" they ask, "Why does this problem keep happening in the first place?"

It's a different kind of leadership muscle. It requires patience. It requires courage. And it requires a bigger view—one that sees not just the crisis in front of you but the patterns underneath it.

When we focus on root causes, we stop spinning in circles. We create lasting solutions that make everything healthier—not just for today but for tomorrow as well. The most effective leaders I know have mastered this balance. They fight today's fires when they must— and they also invest time to understand the fires of tomorrow before they even ignite.

That's what BOLD leadership looks like. It's how you build stronger teams, stronger organizations, and a stronger future—whether you're just leading a department or running the entire company.

The Story of the Five Whys: The Time I Held the Undivided Attention of the Executive Committee

Let me tell you a story that shows exactly why solving the *real* problem— not just the *first* problem—separates good leaders from great ones.

When I stepped into my new role building the customer-relations department (yep, I got the job!), my mission was clear: create a strategy focused on true process improvement, not just Band-Aid solutions. As I prepared to present to the executive committee—a group notorious for being a little distracted and a lot impatient—I knew I needed something that would grab their attention.

That's when I found it: the story of the five whys.

I decided to open with it. And to my amazement, the room got quiet. Every leader leaned in. That story didn't just win their buy-in—it sparked an entire movement inside the company: a new Six Sigma team focused relentlessly on real, lasting change.

Here's the story that grabbed their attention: The Washington Monument was crumbling. The obvious question everyone asked first: "Why is the monument deteriorating?"

Easy: dirt and damage.

Solution? Clean it more. Clean it better. Use different products.

But cleaning didn't solve the problem. In fact, it made it worse. So someone dared to dig deeper:

"Why is it getting so dirty?"

Turns out that it wasn't dirt. It was bird droppings.

So the next fix? Get rid of the birds. Maybe scare them off. Maybe install spikes or fake owls.

But again—someone asked, "Why are the birds even here?"

A little research revealed that the birds were feasting on swarms of insects—midges—drawn to the monument every night.

Another layer deeper: "Why are there so many midges at the monument?"

Because the bright floodlights lit up the night sky—and the insects couldn't resist.

Finally, the question that unlocked everything: "How can we stop the midges?"

Simple: delay turning on the lights until after the insects had moved on for the night.

No bugs. No birds.

The monument stayed cleaner, needed less harsh cleaning, and—bonus—saved money on electricity.

That's the real power of the five whys.

Not settling for the first answer.

Not racing for the quickest fix.

Digging deeper until you find the real root cause—and the real breakthrough.

BOLD leaders know this.

Surface solutions only buy you time.

Root-cause solutions buy you transformation.

If you want lasting change, you have to keep asking the right questions until you get to the root cause and best solution.

Common Challenges in Organizations

Strategies such as the five whys are powerful tools for BOLD leaders, but solving problems effectively requires something even deeper: recognizing the common internal challenges that organizations face before they become full-blown crises. Being proactive isn't just smart leadership; it's essential leadership.

Still, there are some common internal challenges, but BOLD leaders tackle them head-on, including the following:

1. **Lack of Effective Communication**

   Communication breakdowns happen more often than most leaders care to admit—and they come at a brutal cost. Missed deadlines. Duplicated efforts. Projects that stall or fall apart before they even get off the ground. When communication falters, trust erodes. Collaboration weakens. Progress slows to a crawl.

   And it's not just internal. Poor communication with clients, vendors, and partners can do even more damage. Vague updates, unclear expectations, and radio silence create frustration—and eventually, they chip away at your credibility. Clients start questioning your reliability. Vendors stop going the extra mile. The cracks in communication become cracks in your brand.

   BOLD leaders don't wait for the cracks to widen—they address them head-on. They create *communication rhythms* that keep people aligned and moving forward: regular check-ins, structured one-on-ones, proactive outreach to clients and partners. They sharpen their teams' communication skills—active listening, crisp messaging, meaningful feedback—because great communication is a *muscle*, not a memo.

   And they use simple but powerful tools to back it up—project dashboards, collaboration platforms, CRM systems that eliminate confusion and make next steps crystal clear.

In BOLD leadership, communication isn't "nice to have." It's the backbone of execution. Without it, even the best strategies collapse. With it, teams move faster, stronger, and smarter—inside your walls and far beyond them.

2. Overload and Prioritization Issues

Overload is the silent killer of productivity and morale. When everything feels urgent, nothing is prioritized—and the result is a team that's exhausted, directionless, and stuck reacting instead of progressing.

BOLD leaders create clarity. They define and communicate what truly matters, making it easier for their teams to focus energy where it counts most. Assigning tasks based on strengths—not just availability—ensures that work is not only manageable but also meaningful. And the best leaders don't just model prioritization—they equip their teams with it, providing time-management strategies, setting realistic deadlines, and most importantly, empowering people to say no to what doesn't align with the mission. The truth is that discipline in focus is what separates high-performing organizations from the ones that stay stuck spinning their wheels.

3. Leadership Bottlenecks

Leaders can quickly become bottlenecks when they attempt to control all decision-making and micromanage all tasks. This creates many obstacles—not only slowing down processes but also stifling creativity and innovation and demotivating employees. This bottleneck will inevitably cause delays for the team, such that the leader will once again be putting out fires rather than looking ahead to prepare for future challenges and opportunities. BOLD leadership involves trusting and empowering team members to make decisions and take ownership of their work.

Possible solutions could include delegating authority appropriately throughout the team, allowing employees to act and make choices within their areas of expertise, trusting team members to manage their responsibilities, and providing support rather than control to empower them and build trust. With this in place, BOLD leaders can stop focusing on putting out fires and start focusing on strategic planning, concentrating on long-term goals and vision, and guiding the team toward future success.

4. **Insufficient Talent Development and Pipeline**

As organizations grow, leaders need team members who are ready to take on increased responsibilities and leadership roles. Without proper development and succession planning, leaders may lack the necessary talent to support expansion and adapt to new challenges. This may be due to a lack of training opportunities, where they may not have access to the education and experiences needed to develop new skills and competencies, or poor succession planning, where they may not proactively identify and then prepare individuals to fill future key positions.

Possible solutions include investing in professional development with training programs, workshops, and mentorship opportunities to help employees build necessary skills; implementing succession planning to identify potential future leaders; and creating development plans to prepare those future leaders for advanced roles. BOLD leaders often take it a step further by ensuring that continuous learning and development is infused in the organization's culture.

Allow and Reward Failure

What?

Am I actually saying that you should allow and reward failure?

Yes, I sure am!

Why? It encourages innovation and creativity. If employees are afraid to fail, they will not take risks. At best, you will get incremental gains from them. It is when your employees are allowed to innovate without fear that you will see exponential leaps from them. It promotes learning and speed, inspires accountability, builds trust, and sets companies up for success in overcoming complex challenges.

The key is to fail quickly and learn from it. This is where the term "sandbox" comes from in software development. You create a safe environment to test out new features and products where you can conduct experimentation.

Expert tip: when team members try out something new and it doesn't go swimmingly, spend time debriefing to figure out lessons learned and what everyone should take with them on their next step forward.

Certain well-known companies exemplify this: Amazon, Toyota, Netflix, Apple, Dyson, and Pixar. They wouldn't be where they are today had they not failed, repeatedly, on their way to success.

Sara Blakely, CEO of Spanx, grew up in a family where failures were regularly celebrated. Her father would ask this question at the dinner table each night: "What did you fail at today?" He helped see failure as a form of feedback, not as a setback—and as a way to foster creativity and innovation.

Addressing these common obstacles requires BOLD leaders to be proactive with both thoughtful strategies and a commitment to continuous improvement. We don't stay stagnant in fear or in doubt that we can overcome the obstacle. Instead, we examine, learn, formulate our plan, and move forward with confidence.

Leadership Attributes Essential for Overcoming Challenges

Leaders often set a certain plan to move forward. The issue is that sometimes they get so committed to that one plan that they can't see that it isn't working the way they thought it would or that the resources aren't available like they had imagined. Something has changed to cause them to not be able to execute the plan like they assumed they would be able to, and that something is usually an obstacle of some sort. The more they allow themselves to be adaptable and have the flexibility to adjust to change, the better they are. To that end, just like with any other aspect of leadership, certain attributes will help leaders not only overcome challenges but also thrive once they have done so.

BOLD leaders look to excel in the following key areas:

- **Adaptability.** BOLD leaders have the ability to adjust to new circumstances, learn from experiences, and embrace change. Adaptability helps ensure that individuals and organizations can evolve in response to shifting environments, staying relevant and effective in the face of ever-present challenges. The key is knowing when to adapt versus when to stay the course. BOLD leaders don't give up too soon.
- **Perseverance.** The commitment to keep pushing forward, even when faced with prolonged difficulties or repeated failures, is part of having a growth mindset, like BOLD leaders have. Perseverance involves a strong work ethic and determination to see things through to the end, no matter how tough the journey may be. A boss once said to me, "Fail fast so you can figure it out and learn from it." Problems force us to figure things out differently, grow from the process, and learn a valuable lesson.
- **Resilience.** The ability to bounce back from setbacks, stay focused on goals, and maintain a positive attitude, especially in difficult situations, is crucial for overcoming challenges. Resilience helps leaders ensure that challenges don't derail a team's progress but rather become opportunities for growth.
- **Resourcefulness.** BOLD leaders have the capacity to think outside the box and find creative solutions to their problems. They leverage all available resources and collaborate effectively with the team. Resourcefulness allows us to navigate obstacles by using what's at hand in innovative ways.

Obstacles are not roadblocks for BOLD leaders—they're proving grounds. In the spirit of *daring drive*, the leaders who make the biggest impact aren't the ones who avoid adversity; they're the ones who face it head-on, learn from it, and emerge stronger. Every setback, every misstep, every unexpected challenge offers a chance to grow sharper, smarter, and more resilient. It's not about avoiding failure; it's about building the endurance and agility to move through it with courage and conviction. Leaders who pause, ask deeper questions, and find the real root of the problem—not just the surface symptom—are the ones who create lasting change. Daring drive is about choosing growth over fear, strategy over reaction, and transformation over quick fixes. The obstacles you overcome aren't just challenges—they're catalysts for your greatest breakthroughs.

BOLD Takeaways

- **Failure isn't fatal—it's foundational.** Every mistake holds a lesson that makes you and your organization stronger.

- **The best leaders don't just solve problems—they solve the right problems.** Dig deeper. Fix the root cause, not just the surface issue.

- **Adaptability, resilience, and perseverance are your real superpowers.** Stay flexible, stay determined, and keep moving forward when others quit.

- **Empowering others to own challenges strengthens the entire team.** Trust your people, delegate wisely, and build a culture that thrives even when obstacles arise.

Chapter 16:
Drive Through the Difficult Journal Prompts

1. What challenge am I currently facing—and am I reacting or responding?
Where do I need to pause and assess instead of rushing to fix?

2. How often are we identifying the root cause versus just the surface symptom?
What's underneath this issue that keeps it coming back?

3. When was the last time I changed my mind based on new insight?
What did I learn—and what did it unlock?

4. Where can I create more space for my team to fail, learn, and grow?
What messages am I sending about risk, failure, and innovation?

5. Where have I been firefighting instead of fireproofing?
What systems or habits need to change in order to prevent future issues?

6. What's a recent failure I experienced—and what did it teach me?
How can I use that insight to lead better going forward?

7. Who on my team is solving problems at the surface level?
How can I help them go deeper and think more strategically?

8. What's one area where I need to be more intellectually honest?
Where am I holding onto a decision that no longer makes sense?

9. Where am I empowering others to take ownership in tough situations?
What's one step I can take to support—not rescue—someone this week?

10. What strength or navigation method has helped me overcome difficult times?
How can I tap into that now?

What Gets Celebrated Gets Repeated

"No one does great things alone. Success is always a team effort."
—Mary Barra, CEO of GM

In her 2014 commencement speech to the graduating class at the University of Michigan, Mary Barra emphasized that "success is always a team effort," underscoring the importance of collaboration and recognizing collective achievements in effective leadership.[xxxvi] Barra's philosophy highlights that celebrating team successes fosters trust, strengthens relationships, and motivates individuals to perform at their best, making it crucial in driving long-term success at GM and beyond. But what might happen if all that success goes unrecognized?

Leaders often give too much attention to what's wrong instead of reinforcing what is right. Dealing with challenges and achieving success are two experiences that can bond a group of individuals together. But often, leaders and teams get stuck in a cycle of focusing only on what went wrong—who made mistakes, how things went off course, and where improvement is needed. Though addressing challenges is vital in leadership, reflecting on and celebrating the factors that contributed to the successes is paramount. Yet many leaders feel that they need to wait for something big to happen before they should celebrate and therefore miss the opportunity to reward the critical milestones of progress.

Recognition doesn't diminish motivation—it fuels it.

Fear of Recognition?

I once worked under a leader who, while competent and well intentioned, struggled with giving recognition. His fear was that praising people too much would cause them to ease up—believing they had "arrived" and no longer needed to push as hard. Instead of fueling momentum, he worried that it would kill it.

The unintended consequence? Our days felt transactional. We showed up, worked hard, and left—with little acknowledgment of the effort, growth, or wins along the way. Over time, uncertainty crept in. Without feedback, team members were left to wonder: *Am I doing a good job? Am I valued here?* Fear, doubt, and disengagement quietly took root.

During one of our regular one-on-ones, I brought this up. He had noticed that I often celebrated wins within my team—and he was curious, even skeptical, about whether that was the right approach. He shared his concern that too much recognition might make people complacent.

I saw it differently. Experience—and leadership research—taught me this: recognition doesn't slow people down; it accelerates them. Recognition fuels motivation. It reinforces what's working. It builds trust, confidence, and pride. Far from making people complacent, authentic acknowledgment inspires them to reach even higher.

BOLD leadership understands this truth: celebrating success isn't a distraction from performance; it's the engine that powers it.

The Importance of Recognition

According to studies by Gallup and HR Daily Advisor, consistent recognition helps employees stay motivated and aligned with organizational goals, enhancing productivity and fostering continuous improvement. It creates positive momentum, with employees feeling valued for their efforts, which keeps them striving toward future milestones.[xxxvii]

When employees don't regularly receive recognition, they often become disengaged, uncertain if their efforts are contributing meaningfully. This disengagement can increase burnout and the likelihood of turnover, with research revealing that companies without recognition programs see significantly higher voluntary turnover. Gallup found that well-recognized employees are 45 percent less likely to have turned over two years later.[xxxviii] Recognition, therefore, is not just a "nice to have" but a strategic tool that sustains retention and performance. Employees who feel appreciated are more likely to remain loyal, productive, and motivated to contribute, while organizations with robust recognition systems experience improved morale and lower turnover rates.

BOLD leaders understand that positive interactions and recognition are essential for fostering a healthy work environment. Employees need to know that their work matters, not only to see the impact of their efforts but to stay motivated to push through challenges. When leaders provide timely and meaningful recognition, they build trust and promote collaboration, creating a culture where people feel connected and supported. In such environments, individuals thrive because they know that they are valued, and teams become stronger, more resilient, and better equipped to achieve long-term success.

Recognition motivates people to work even harder. It's like watering a flower: you see people perk up when you give them positive feedback, and they want to keep excelling so they can get more hydration. They don't feel that because they were celebrated, the work is over. There will always be more goals to achieve, more milestones to hit, and more tasks to be accomplished. And when someone feels good about being recognized for their hard work, it's fuel to keep them moving forward, and their desire to experience it again is strong. The motivation doesn't end—to the contrary, it's actually fueled by positive reinforcement. I think of it like a ladder: the more you recognize and reinforce your team members as they climb, the more confidence they will gain and continue their climb to the top.

"How?" you ask? The best way is for leaders to celebrate the small wins that lead to bigger successes. BOLD leaders acknowledge these moments when progress is being made to keep the team motivated along the way. When we shift our attention to what the team did well, it not only boosts morale but creates a learning environment where the right behaviors are reinforced. Celebrate what you want to see more of.

Alternatively, waiting until the end of a project to celebrate can have significant negative consequences. Large projects span months or even years, and without periodic recognition of progress, teams can feel drained and demotivated. Fatigue sets in and they slightly decrease their pace or time. It may not even be noticeable at first, but over time, the incremental losses start to mount and leaders might ask themselves, "How did this train get so far off the tracks?"

The social exchange theory (SET), developed by sociologist Peter Blau in 1964, provides a framework for understanding how relationships between individuals or between individuals and organizations are influenced by reciprocal exchanges of resources.[xxxix] In the context of workplace relationships, SET suggests that employees expect a degree of reciprocity from their organization: when they invest effort, time, and dedication, they anticipate some form of acknowledgment or reward in return.[xl] When team members lose sight of the bigger picture and feel that their hard work is going unnoticed and unappreciated, it builds resentment and entitlement. Celebrating incremental wins (not everything all the time) along the way helps sustain momentum and ensures that the team remains engaged and energized throughout the process.

Recognition: The Fuel for Winning Cultures

Recognition is one of the most powerful motivators in leadership—and too often, it's underestimated. Though some individuals may shrug off praise, claiming that they don't need it, the reality is that almost everyone thrives when their efforts are seen and appreciated. BOLD leaders know that recognition isn't a luxury—it's a necessity. And it's not one-size-fits-all. Some team members crave public acknowledgment; others prefer a quiet, sincere thank-you behind the scenes. Part of leading BOLDly is learning how each person likes to be recognized and delivering it in a way that resonates.

Here's the trap that many leaders fall into: pushing endlessly toward the next milestone without ever pausing to celebrate the progress made. When teams operate at a breakneck pace without stopping to acknowledge success, burnout creeps in. The finish line always seems to move further away, leaving people feeling like they can never catch up—and worse, like their effort isn't enough. Even for team members who aren't highly driven "achievers," the absence of recognition can be exhausting and demoralizing. Over time, it erodes motivation, drains energy, and makes it feel like the work will never be sustainable.

Recognition isn't just about boosting individual morale; it's the glue that builds strong, winning cultures. Celebrating wins reinforces the behaviors you want to see, strengthens belonging, and fuels pride in the team and the mission. It sends a powerful message: You matter. Your work matters. We're winning together.

I've seen the effects of both approaches firsthand.

When I led a sizable region for a Fortune 500 company, we kicked off every week with a senior-leadership forecast call. The Monday Morning Commit was originally aimed at removing obstacles and driving results. But what it actually became was a draining ritual of critiques and detailed deal micromanagement. Hit four out of five goals?

THE BEATINGS WILL CONTINUE UNTIL MORALE IMPROVES

The call focused relentlessly on the one that was missed, no matter the actual impact or importance. "Why didn't you do this? Why didn't you do that? Why don't you have the details of every single opportunity in your pipeline?" It was a beatdown disguised as problem-solving. And the ones who seemed to have all of the answers all the time were simply making shit up. I used to bemoan that the headline of the call would be "The beatings will continue until morale improves." Not exactly the energy you want to launch into a new week with!

The fallout was real: lower morale, risk avoidance, and innovation suffocated under the weight of constant scrutiny. Despite smart strategies and steady growth, you couldn't help but wonder, *How much more could we have achieved if we focused more on what was going right, what was most impactful and fueled the team with recognition, not just relentless pressure?*

In contrast, at another company, recognition was woven into the culture. We worked hard—and celebrated even harder. Big wins meant T-shirts, team lunches, sometimes even a giant inflatable gorilla on the roof. It wasn't about the prizes. It was about the feeling: we are building something important together. The difference in morale, performance, and loyalty was undeniable.

BOLD leaders understand this simple truth: Recognition isn't a distraction from performance. It's the engine that drives it.

Be BOLD

In *The Leadership Challenge*, James Kouzes and Barry Posner emphasize that one of the most powerful practices of effective leadership is "encouraging the heart." Great leaders understand that recognition doesn't have to come in grand gestures or flashy rewards. It's about something much deeper: making people feel seen, valued, and genuinely appreciated. Kouzes and Posner highlight that the most impactful recognition is personal, specific, and heartfelt. It's not about formality; it's about connection.

I attended a leadership meeting where James Kouzes was the guest speaker. I had just finished reading his book and, had I known he would be speaking, would've brought my copy for him to sign. After his inspiring talk, I had the chance to meet him personally. I shared how much his work had influenced my views on leadership and personal growth. When I mentioned that I didn't have my book with me, he graciously handed me his card and told me to email him—he'd send me a signed copy. I was thrilled.

Later, reflecting on how much his message would resonate with my team, I asked if he would sign 10 copies so I could gift them to my peer group. I offered to purchase them, of course. He responded with a kind and encouraging note: "I'm sure your boldness serves you well in leadership." He arranged everything, and when the books arrived, I opened mine to find a message that stopped me in my tracks:

"Kim, you are my role model for encouraging the heart. You make an extraordinary difference in the lives of so many."

That moment wasn't just a highlight—it was a vivid reminder of how deeply meaningful personal recognition can be.

James's encouragement to "be BOLD" wasn't just a kind gesture—it was a powerful validation that leadership is about much more than delivering results. It's about building people up along the way. His example reinforced my belief that leadership is most powerful when it's personal, human, and heart-centered.

Encouraging the heart isn't an extra task. It's core to leadership. It's what transforms teams from good to great, from compliant to committed. And it's something every BOLD leader can practice—every single day.

The Lasting Impact of Celebration

The key to thriving, both individually and as a team, lies in understanding what makes success happen—and then doing more of it. When leaders focus on studying and building on what's working, they create powerful momentum for even greater achievements.

Imagine a team that, instead of spending all its time dissecting failures, takes time to study and celebrate what went right. They dig into the strategies, innovations, communication methods, and workflows that led to wins—and then replicate and scale them. This shift in mindset transforms reflection into a growth engine. Success isn't a lucky accident; it becomes a blueprint for future victories.

BOLD leaders know that celebrating success isn't about handing out trophies or throwing an occasional party. It's about strengthening relationships, building trust, and creating a culture where people feel deeply valued for their contributions. When people feel recognized, they naturally take more initiative, stretch further, and stay engaged longer.

Celebrating success also creates a powerful feedback loop. Recognition fuels motivation, which drives even bigger results, which leads to even more recognition. It builds an energy that lifts performance across the board—and creates a team environment where people want to stay and grow.

Importantly, you don't have to wait until the final goal is achieved in order to celebrate.

Expert tip: Celebrate the journey—the milestones, the breakthroughs, the moments of grit. Recognize progress as much as outcomes, inspiring teams to keep pushing toward even greater heights.

When we celebrate success intentionally, we don't just acknowledge what's been achieved—we unlock what's possible.

Finding Balance in Celebrations

Leaders often grapple with finding the right balance between recognizing progress frequently enough to keep motivation high and avoiding overdoing it to the point where praise feels meaningless. This was a challenge my former supervisor faced, concerned that too much recognition would lead to complacency. It's a common fear I hear from leaders we coach. They'll say things like, "It seems ridiculous to celebrate what I consider table stakes—like an employee showing up on time or making a few calls." I completely agree. Showing up on time and being prepared is essential, but these behaviors don't necessarily warrant constant celebration. However, acknowledging them occasionally helps employees see that such habits are noticed and valued.

The real power of recognition is in noticing when people are doing things that align with team goals—catching them in the act of doing something right and showing how their efforts make a difference to the team's success. Recognizing meaningful contributions helps clarify what's expected, offers guidance on how to improve, and motivates people to stay on track. When recognition is specific and tied to key behaviors, it not only reinforces those actions but also builds a shared understanding of what success looks like for everyone.

Being specific is the key to making recognition effective. Here's an example:

- Less-effective recognition: "Great job, Megan! Way to go!"
- More-effective recognition: "Megan, the analysis you put together for the supply-chain process improvement was insightful and valuable. You helped us get to the root cause of the issues instead of just fixing the symptoms. Your work is making a real impact, adding $50,000 to the bottom line! Plus, the way you got your peers on board with the next steps has set us up for success. Awesome job!"

Both examples are recognition, but the second one is way more powerful. It gives Megan a clear sense of what she did right so she can keep doing it. The first example, though nice, is too vague—it doesn't really help her understand what she did well or how to repeat it.

Capture the Lead

One of the most effective ways to fuel recognition is by tying celebrations to meaningful milestones—especially lead indicators. These small, early wins pave the way to bigger goals. For example, if strengthening client relationships is a strategic priority, don't just wait to celebrate the final contract signing. Recognize the successful first meeting, the breakthrough conversation, or the moment that a new level of trust is built. These milestones signal real momentum and energize the team for the journey ahead.

When done thoughtfully, recognition isn't just about rewarding outcomes—it's about honoring the behaviors and progress that drive results. BOLD leaders who master this create cultures where people feel seen, appreciated, and connected to something bigger than themselves. Recognition becomes more than a moment of applause; it becomes a catalyst for engagement, performance, and loyalty. Research consistently shows that employees who feel valued are more motivated, more productive, and more likely to stay. Recognition, when woven into the rhythm of an organization, becomes a powerful lever for building a high-performing, future-focused team.

Recognition isn't a luxury; it's leadership rocket fuel. In today's fast-paced, results-driven world, it's easy to skip the celebration and rush to the next challenge. But BOLD leaders know that recognizing progress—early, often, and meaningfully—builds the energy, trust, and momentum needed for extraordinary results. Recognition fuels motivation, strengthens team connection, and creates a culture where people want to show up and give their best. It's not about waiting for grand achievements—it's about celebrating the climb, reinforcing the right behaviors, and making success sustainable, not exhausting. When leaders make recognition part of their rhythm, they unlock deeper engagement, greater loyalty, and bigger wins across the board.

BOLD Takeaways

- **Recognition fuels momentum.** Small wins celebrated along the way inspire bigger achievements and sustained effort.

- **Failure to recognize leads to burnout.** Teams that feel unseen will eventually lose energy, engagement, and trust.

- **Tailored, specific praise builds stronger teams.** Personalizing recognition and tying it to meaningful contributions amplifies its impact.

- **Celebrating success is not optional.** It's a strategic leadership practice that multiplies loyalty, performance, and long-term growth.

Chapter 17:
What Gets Celebrated Gets Repeated
Journal Prompts

1. What and who on my team deserves recognition right now but hasn't received it?
What have they done recently that's moved the mission forward?

2. How am I celebrating small wins along the way—not just the finish line?
What moments of progress have I overlooked?

3. How can I ensure that I tailor recognition to each individual's preferences?
Who prefers public praise? Who values a quiet thank-you?

4. When was the last time I reinforced the right behavior with specific praise?
What message did I send with my feedback?

5. Where do I have more opportunity to recognize lead indicators?
What early behaviors or signals deserve celebration?

6. How often do I pause to reflect on what's going well?
What's working—and how can I do more of it?

7. What fears or misconceptions do I have about over-recognizing?
Where might I be holding back when I should be leaning in?

8. How does my team know that they're making a difference?
Where do I need to connect their effort to our impact?

9. What system or rhythm can I create to build recognition into my leadership habits?
What would weekly, intentional celebrations look like?

10. Who has celebrated me—and how did it make me feel?
What can I learn from that to pay it forward?

Chapter 18

The Journey to BOLD Leadership

As with any journey, in bringing this BOLD leadership guide to a close, it's essential to stop and reflect on what we've explored and the lessons learned along the way. BOLD leadership is not a static destination but rather a dynamic, evolving process. It's an adventure filled with as many moments of triumph, success, and satisfaction as those of challenge, discomfort, and growth. It is the culmination of all those moments that shape us into a BOLD leader capable of making a significant, long-term impact.

The lessons within these pages stem from my journey—filled with successes and hard-earned lessons, as well as the wisdom shared by other leaders I've studied, worked for, and worked with. As I mentioned in the introduction, my story began with several profound professional setbacks and the harsh realization that so many times, I wasn't yet the leader I aspired to be. I struggled with confidence, vision, knowledge, and the support needed to lead BOLDly in those early days. Yet precisely in those difficult moments is when I uncovered insights that would forever transform my leadership path and help others transform theirs.

Throughout this book, we've examined the elements of BOLD leadership: brilliant vision, oneness/ownership, lighthouse leadership, and daring drive. They were chosen for a reason. Intentionally combined, these pillars create a strong foundation for success. That's because true leadership is more than just checking boxes or following a rigid formula. It's more than managing tasks or telling others what to do. It's evolving with your experiences, learning from your mistakes, and cultivating the courage to step into the unknown—all of which occur within these pillars. As I said, it's an adventure!

BOLD Leadership in Practice

BOLD leadership is intentional. Throughout this book, we've explored the framework of BOLD leadership in each of the four parts, and now it's time to bring it all together. Here's a recap of what it means to lead with BOLDness:

- **Brilliant Vision:** Your vision is the compass that guides your leadership. You don't want to merely set goals, but rather, you want to create a vivid, inspiring picture of what success looks like for you and your team. A brilliant vision pushes you to think bigger, innovate, dream beyond the status quo, and inspire others to enroll in the vision as well.
- **Oneness/Ownership**: Leadership is at its best when you are self-aware, intentional, and authentic. The best leaders know this and continually invest in their development, learning lessons and applying this new knowledge in order to continue to grow and improve. The strongest platform for leadership is the one that comes directly from you—from listening to yourself, self-reflection, and honing your talents so you can be at your best.
- **Lighthouse Leadership:** Just like a lighthouse guiding ships in, leaders are beacons of light in times of uncertainty. A lighthouse leader provides clarity, direction, and reassurance, especially when the path forward is unclear. This kind of leadership requires consistency and transparency, even when the navigation is difficult.
- **Daring Drive:** BOLD leaders are driven by a desire to achieve greatness. They have the courage to take risks, challenge the status quo, and enable their teams to go beyond what they thought possible. Daring drive isn't just ambition; it's consistent efforts, perseverance, and grit in the face of adversity.

These four elements are the pillars of BOLD leadership. When you integrate them into your leadership practice, along with resilience and authenticity, you unlock the potential to lead others with purpose, passion, and impact.

The Role of Resilience in BOLD Leadership

As we more fully explored in the previous chapter, resilience is truly the cornerstone of BOLD leadership. Every leader will face setbacks—whether it's a failed initiative, a personal disappointment, or an external challenge outside their control. These moments can feel defeating, but they also hold the greatest opportunities for growth when we are resilient.

Take me, for example, when I didn't receive the promotion I was so sure I'd earned. It felt like the end of the road. We've all worked with many leaders who have similar stories, but that setback became a huge turning point for me and my career. It forced me to confront my insecurities, ego, and limitations as a leader. Looking back, it wasn't getting the promotion that would have made me a better leader. It was the journey through self-discovery after **not** getting it that did. That journey is what led me down the path to becoming a BOLD leader.

I have since realized that resilience isn't just about bouncing back, as many people tend to think. It's about bouncing forward. With resilience, every challenge is an invitation to learn more about yourself, your team, and the path you want to take. When I embraced this mindset, I found the courage to be vulnerable, admit my shortcomings, prioritize, be more intentional, and, probably most importantly, ask for help when I needed it—not an easy feat for most. In doing so, I built stronger, more authentic connections with my team and gained the confidence to lead with clarity and conviction.

Authentically BOLD Leadership

If you take only one thing with you on your BOLD leadership journey, let it be this: authenticity is key to effective leadership. Early in my career, I tried to mold myself into what I had witnessed and thought others wanted. I was moving fast and emulating both some good and bad behaviors. At times, I prioritized being liked and pleasing people over being true to myself. This backfired, leading only to indecisiveness, ambiguity, and, ultimately, less-than-stellar leadership.

The more I tried to be someone I wasn't, the more disconnected I became from my vision and purpose. It wasn't until I spent time gathering feedback and reflecting that I was able to embrace my authentic self. That is when I started to see real progress in my leadership. Authenticity is what allows you to connect deeply with others and build trust—a fundamental element of BOLD leadership.

In embracing authenticity, I also learned the importance of leading from my strengths rather than focusing solely on my weaknesses.

Expert tip: rather than pouring all your energy into improving your weaknesses, invest in what you're naturally good at and watch it flourish.

When you lead from your strengths, you bring a unique energy and passion to your work that is contagious. When you work in your Zone of Genius, your ability to thrive is unsurpassed.

Your team will see it, feel it, and be inspired by it.

Leadership Is an Adventure

Why do I call leadership a "BOLD adventure"? Because it is exactly that: a thrilling journey that pushes you out of your comfort zone and into uncharted territory on nearly a daily basis. Leadership is full of twists and turns, obstacles, and triumphs. BOLD leaders embrace uncertainty and take risks. We pursue big dreams with the knowledge that things won't always go according to plan. I can't think of a better word to use than "adventure" to describe it.

Adventure comes with its share of challenges, but that's what makes it so rewarding. As I've shared, some of the most profound lessons I've learned as a leader came from my greatest challenges. From navigating difficult relationships with colleagues and managing a team through impossible deadlines to learning how to communicate better and exemplify the leadership traits I wanted to see in others, the challenges forced me to grow in ways I never imagined.

As BOLD leaders, we must learn to embrace the discomfort that comes with growth. My niece Grace put it best when she said, "You should do something every day that makes you uncomfortable." This wisdom couldn't be truer for leadership. Every day presents an opportunity to stretch yourself, take a risk, and step into the unknown. When you do this consistently, you unlock potential in yourself and your team that you didn't know was possible—an adventure in and of itself!

The Ripple Effect of BOLD Leadership

Leadership creates a ripple effect. The way you lead impacts not only your immediate team but also your organization, your community, and the people around you. This ripple effect can be either positive or negative, depending on the choices you make and the actions you take. BOLD leadership ensures that the ripple effect is a power for good.

Throughout my career, I've seen firsthand how leadership decisions can either inspire and motivate or create frustration and disengagement. As BOLD leaders, we have a tremendous responsibility to create the former: positive ripples. This means leading with integrity, authenticity, and BOLDness. It means empowering others to be their best selves and providing the guidance and support they need to do just that.

The best part is that when you lead with BOLDness, you inspire others to be bold too. You create an environment where people feel safe to take risks, make mistakes, and grow. You build a culture of trust, innovation, and collaboration. And ultimately, you leave a legacy of positive impact that extends far beyond your tenure as a leader.

A Call to Action: Be the Rising Tide

Leadership is not easy, and it's not for the faint of heart. But it is one of the most rewarding adventures you will ever embark upon. When you lead with BOLDness, you open yourself up to new possibilities, deeper connections, and greater impact. As you move forward in your leadership journey, remember that becoming a BOLD leader is not about perfection; it's about progress. It's about learning from your mistakes, celebrating your wins, and staying committed to your vision even when the path is unclear.

In concluding this book, my message to you, all leaders, is simple: be the rising tide that lifts all boats. You have an opportunity to make a lasting, positive impact, not only on your organization but also on everyone around you. Strive to be your best and lift those around you. You are a light, a guide, and an example of what leadership should look like. Please don't take that responsibility lightly. Others need that light in order to achieve their own greatness.

The path ahead will likely be filled with as many challenges as successes, but it will also be filled with growth and discovery. Stay curious, stay resilient, and stay true to yourself. Be BOLD in your vision, BOLD in your decisions, and BOLD in your belief that you can achieve greatness.

I leave you with this final thought. Being BOLD leaders does not mean we are fearless. It means that we are brave enough to face our fears and lead anyway. It means that we take risks, embrace uncertainty, and dare to dream bigger than most others could have ever imagined.

So be BOLD, fellow leaders. The world needs you.

Acknowledgments

Let's be honest: writing a book is not for the faint of heart. This particular endeavor took many years and had several stops and starts. It's a lot like leadership—romanticized from a distance, frequently chaotic up close, and almost always accompanied by a voice in your head asking, *Who thought this was a good idea?* But I persevered and did it anyway—because leadership matters—A LOT! When leaders are better, everyone benefits. Teams thrive. Organizations grow. Families and communities feel the ripple. And if this book contributes even one drop to that ripple effect, it's worth every messy, magical moment that it took to get here.

First, to the **incredible leaders** I've had the honor of working alongside—you are the heartbeat of this book. I've partnered with some of the most brilliant, creative, complex, driven, and occasionally delightfully difficult people out there. You've inspired me, challenged me, taught me, and reminded me that BOLD leadership isn't about perfection—it's about showing up, standing up, staying open to the lessons, picking yourself back up and ultimately doing the right thing, even when it's wildly inconvenient and appears there is no positive end in sight. Thank you for being real and for giving me a front-row seat to your leadership journeys.

To **Amelia Forczak**, **Deanna Novak**, and the sharp strategic team at **Pithy Wordsmithery**—you helped pull this across the finish line without a single dramatic rescue helicopter. From shaping chapters to refining the final manuscript, your partnership has been a master class in clarity, persistence, and good judgment (especially when I had none). Thank you for elevating the ideas, wrangling the chaos, and helping keep me to the timelines (mostly!).

To **Sarah Victory**, thank you for dreaming up the title and original concept of this book. Your foresight and encouragement helped launch this adventure before I even realized how big the mountain was. And **Dan Gershenson**, thank you for showing up early in the journey with structure, creativity, and patience. You helped translate scattered thoughts into actual sentences—I'm forever grateful.

To **my incredible team at Aspiration Catalyst®**—you believed in this message long before it had a table of contents. Thank you for living the BOLD values, holding me accountable, and keeping the lights on while I disappeared into writing mode. You are the backbone of this work and proof that leadership starts with a strong team.

To my many **peers, mentors, clients, and colleagues**—thank you for your trust, honesty, and willingness to engage in difficult conversations. Your experiences, questions, and bold moves are stitched through these pages. This is your book as much as it is mine.

To my **friends and family**—thank you for your grace, humor, and unwavering support through every "I just need to finish one more section" and "No, it's still not done." Your patience and encouragement carried me more than you know. So many of you checked in, cheered me on, and reminded me to keep going. You know who you are, and I'm forever grateful for your belief in me and in this wild, wonderful journey.

To **my mom**, who consistently encouraged me to go in the direction of strength, and lead.

And to **my dad**, who showed me what patient and steadfast leadership looks like, and who once said, "Honey, they call it work for a reason"—your dry wit lives rent-free in my head.

But in all seriousness, I will encourage everyone not to let that be your answer. Your work, your leadership, your purpose—it should mean something. So choose with intention. Lead with courage. Be a positive force in our world. Let the power you hold be a lighthouse—steady, strong, and unmistakably BOLD. And as you rise, lift others with you. That's what leadership is meant to be.

To BOLD leaders everywhere, may your ripple reach far.

About the Author

Kim Svoboda is a BOLD leader, seasoned tech executive, and unapologetic intrapreneur-turned-entrepreneur. As the founder and CEO of Aspiration Catalyst®, she's spent the last decade helping leaders ditch excuses, crush goals, and build high-performing teams that actually perform. Her firm partners with top companies to develop BOLD leaders who lead with clarity, courage, and conviction—because when leaders are better, everyone benefits.

Before launching her own firm, Kim spent 25+ years thriving in the fast-paced world of Fortune 500 technology giants like Adobe, CDW, Insight Enterprises, and UScellular, where she led teams, built divisions from scratch, and held P&L responsibility up to $1B. She built businesses from zero to millions—often while navigating change, skepticism, and the thrilling chaos of growth. As an intrapreneur, she was the one raising her hand to ask, "Why not?"—then rolling up her sleeves to figure it out.

Kim founded **Aspiration Catalyst®** with one BOLD mission: to empower leaders to lead with courage; build excuse-proof, goal-crushing teams; and drive results—with heart, not ego. Ten years later, it has grown into a powerhouse collective of **seasoned executive coaches** who bring a rare combination of **real-world business experience, sharp strategic thinking, and a deep understanding of human dynamics**.

Our coaches have sat in the executive seats—they've led teams, launched products, grown businesses, navigated M&A, and managed P&Ls. They've worked in fast-paced, high-pressure environments and understand the complexity that leaders face today. Each brings their own industry expertise—from tech to finance, healthcare to manufacturing—but all share a commitment to pushing leaders forward, not holding their hands. They don't rely on theory alone. They bring bold questions, honest feedback, and practical tools that translate to real-world results.

Aspiration Catalyst® partners with **private-equity firms, technology companies, professional-services firms, financial institutions, healthcare systems, manufacturers, government agencies, and associations**. Whether guiding a CEO through transformation, helping senior leaders align post-merger, or developing high-potential managers into confident, accountable leaders, our coaches meet leaders where they are—and push them to where they need to be.

Kim serves as chair of the board of directors for the BBB of Chicago and is on the board of advisors for the Executives' Club of Chicago. She's also an award-winning keynote speaker, a certified executive coach (ICF, Gallup, and E2Grow), and a voice in some of the most influential leadership forums in the country.

Outside of work, Kim is a triathlete, a passionate advocate for community and ethics, and a lover of live music and big adventures. In 2015, she and her family packed their bags, circled the globe, and explored five continents and 26 countries—many of them inspired by years of reading *National Geographic* and one particular article in *O, The Oprah Magazine*, about a family traveling around the world together. The trip changed their lives and reaffirmed Kim's belief that leadership isn't about control—it's about curiosity, courage, and creating something bigger than yourself.

BOLD Leadership is her first book and a powerful call to lead true, lead strong, and lift others every step of the way.

Reading List:

The 7 Habits of Highly Effective People by Stephen Covey

The One Minute Manager by Kenneth Blanchard and Spencer Johnson

Raving Fans: A Revolutionary Approach to Customer Service by Kenneth Blanchard and Sheldon Bowles

Who Moved My Cheese? by Spencer Johnson, MD

Multipliers: How the Best Leaders Make Everyone Smarter by Liz Wiseman and Greg McKeown

Emotional Intelligence 2.0 by Travis Bradberry and Jean Greaves

Good to Great: Why Some Companies Make the Leap...and Others Don't by Jim Collins

The Compound Effect: Jumpstart Your Income, Your Life, Your Success by Darren Hardy

Atomic Habits: An Easy & Proven Way to Build Good Habits & Break Bad Ones by James Clear

Grit: The Power of Passion and Perseverance by Angela Duckworth

Essentialism: The Disciplined Pursuit of Less by Greg McKeown

StrengthsFinder 2.0 by Tom Rath and Donald O. Clifton

Exploring Positive Relationships at Work: Building a Theoretical and Research Foundation edited by Jane E. Dutton and Belle Rose Ragins

The Let Them Theory: A Life-Changing Tool That Millions of People Can't Stop Talking About by Mel Robbins

Conversational Intelligence: How Great Leaders Build Trust and Get Extraordinary Results by Judith E. Glaser

The Genius Zone: The Breakthrough Process to End Negative Thinking and Live in True Creativity by Dr. Gay Hendricks

The Marriage Clinic: A Scientifically Based Marital Therapy by John M. Gottman

Start with Why: How Great Leaders Inspire Everyone to Take Action by Simon Sinek

It's the Manager: Moving from Boss to Coach by Jim Clifton and Jim Harter

Tuesdays with Morrie by Mitch Albom

Radical Candor: Be a Kick-Ass Boss Without Losing Your Humanity by Kim Scott

Dare to Lead: Brave Work. Tough Conversations. Whole Hearts by Brené Brown

The Leadership Challenge: How to Make Extraordinary Things Happen in Organizations by James Kouzes and Barry Posner

What Got You Here Won't Get You There by Marshall Goldsmith

The Productivity Project: Accomplishing More by Managing Your Time, Attention, and Energy Better by Chris Bailey

10x Is Easier Than 2x: How World-Class Entrepreneurs Achieve More by Doing Less by Dan Sullivan and Dr. Benjamin Hardy

Mindset: The New Psychology of Success by Dr. Carol S. Dweck

Who Not How: The Formula to Achieve Bigger Goals Through Accelerating Teamwork by Dan Sullivan and Dr. Benjamin Hardy

Exchange and Power in Social Life by Peter M. Blau

Endnotes

i   George A. Miller, "The Magical Number Seven, Plus or Minus Two: Some Limits on Our Capacity for Processing Information," *Psychological Review* 63, no. 2 (1956): 81.

ii   "Developing New Managers? How to Set Your First-Time Leaders Up for Success," Center for Creative Leadership (August 16, 2022), https://www.ccl.org/articles/leading-effectively-articles/prepare-first-time-leaders-success/.

iii   "Journal of Experimental Psychology: General, American Psychological Association," https://www.apa.org/pubs/journals/xge.

iv   Hal E. Hershfield et al., "Increasing Saving Behavior Through Age-Progressed Renderings of the Future Self," *National Library of Medicine* 48, https://pmc.ncbi.nlm.nih.gov/articles/PMC3949005/, https://www.anderson.ucla.edu/documents/areas/fac/marketing/Hershfield_Goldstein_Sharpe_Fox_Yeykelis_Carstensen_Bailenson_2011_JMR.pdf?utm_source=chatgpt.com.

v   *Ibid.*

vi   Darren Hardy, *The Compound Effect: Jumpstart Your Income, Your Life, Your Success* (New York: Vanguard Press, 2010); James Clear, *Atomic Habits: An Easy & Proven Way to Build Good Habits & Break Bad Ones* (New York: Avery, 2018); Angela Duckworth, *Grit: The Power of Passion and Perseverance* (New York: Scribner, 2016); Greg McKeown, *Essentialism: The Disciplined Pursuit of Less* (New York: Crown Business, 2014).

vii   Tom Rath and Donald O. Clifton, *StrengthsFinder 2.0* (New York: Gallup Press, 2007).

viii *Ibid.*

ix   *Ibid.*

x   Arran Caza and Jacoba M. Lilius, "The Role of Resilience in Leadership," in *Exploring Positive Relationships at Work: Building a Theoretical and Research Foundation*, ed. Jane E. Dutton and Belle Rose Ragins (New York: Routledge, 2007), 296.

xi   Mel Robbins, *The Let Them Theory: A Life-Changing Tool That Millions of People Can't Stop Talking About* (New York: Hay House, 2024), 106.

xii   Dr. Gay Hendricks, *The Genius Zone: The Breakthrough Process to End Negative Thinking and Live in True Creativity* (New York: St. Martin's Essentials, 2021).

xiii John M. Gottman, *The Marriage Clinic: A Scientifically Based Marital Therapy* (New York: W.W. Norton & Company, 1999), 57.

xiv Simon Sinek, *Start with Why: How Great Leaders Inspire Everyone to Take Action* (New York: Portfolio, 2009).

xv   "Employee Engagement on the Rise in the U.S.," *Gallup*, August 26, 2020, https://www.gallup.com/workplace/285674/improve-employee-engagement-workplace.aspx.

xvi   Jim Clifton and Jim Harter, *It's the Manager: Moving from Boss to Coach* (New York: Gallup Press, 2019).

xvii   *Ibid., 80.*

xviii   Kim Scott, *Radical Candor: Be a Kick-Ass Boss Without Losing Your Humanity* (New York: St. Martin's Press, 2017).

xix   Brené Brown, *Dare to Lead: Brave Work. Tough Conversations. Whole Hearts.* (New York: Random House, 2018), 70.

xx   "legacy" definition, Merriam-Webster online, https://www.merriam-webster .com/dictionary/legacy.

xxi   Greg McKeown, *Essentialism: The Disciplined Pursuit of Less* (New York: Crown Currency, 2014), https://gregmckeown.com/books/essentialism/.

xxii   Albert L. Winseman, D. Min., "The Achiever Theme: How to Productively Aim Your CliftonStrengths Talent," CliftonStrengths, February 12, 2018, https:// www.gallup.com/cliftonstrengths/en/249929/achiever-theme-productively -aim-your-cliftonstrengths-talent.aspx#:~:text=Achiever%20is%20a%20 productivity%20theme,accomplished%20each%20and%20every%20day.

xxiii   "Speaking of Psychology: Why our attention spans are shrinking, with Gloria Mark, PhD," American Psychological Association podcast, Episode 2225, https://www.apa.org/news/podcasts/speaking-of-psychology/attention-spans.

xxiv   Stacey Lastoe, "This Is Nuts: It Takes Nearly 30 Minutes to Refocus After You Get Distracted," The Muse, June 19, 2020, https://www.themuse.com/advice/ this-is-nuts-it-takes-nearly-30-minutes-to-refocus -after-you-get-distracted.

xxv   Manoush Zomorodi et al., "So much sitting, looking at screens. Can we combat our sedentary lives?" NPR, October 3, 2023, https://www.npr.org/2023/ 10/03/1200611617/one-prescription-for-reversing-the-effects-of-daily -binge-sitting-at-your-desk.

xxvi   Darren Hardy, Insane Productivity website, https://insaneproductivity.com/.

xxvii   *Ibid.*

xxviii   Carol S. Dweck, *Mindset: The New Psychology of Success* (New York: Ballantine Books, 2006).

xxix   *Ibid.*

xxx   Dan Sullivan and Dr. Benjamin Hardy, *Who Not How: The Formula to Achieve Bigger Goals Through Accelerating Teamwork* (Carlsbad: Hay House Business, 2020).

xxxi   Jensen Huang, "If You Want to Be Successful, I Would Encourage You to Grow a Tolerance for Failure," interview by Jon Erlichman, YouTube video at 1:45, February 21, 2024.

xxxii   *Ibid.*

xxxiii   *Ibid.*

xxxiv   *Ibid.*

xxxv   Jing Pan, "'Fail quickly and inexpensively': Nvidia founder and CEO Jensen Huang shares his mantra for success — here's why Jim Cramer calls him a bigger visionary than Elon Musk," Yahoo! Finance, February 27, 2024, https://finance.yahoo.com/news/fail-quickly-inexpensively-nvidia-founder-130300123.html?guccounter=1&guce_referrer=aHR0cHM6Ly93d3cuZ29vZ2xlLmNvbS88&guce_referrer_sig=AQAAAGSadG9zMH3b8aKBEhG-00lfYBGEDMDmzBiV01yVRDnySYKg4memuSppFcIAF8jpFd9qaf9zXza4u0CjJqhRUzPado7P7IBczHZZ5GEkyYBwp9GeZle8jeVuaVHu5T-xZgdVWZjTc5mSyUQTaoAHWu36kYDz6uwUWk8kOVzFOMP8.

xxxvi Mary Barra, Commencement Speech at University of Michigan (2014), Best Graduation Speeches, https://www.bestgraduationspeeches.com/mary-barra-speech-university-of-michigan-transcript-quotes-video/.

xxxvii "The Human-Centered Workplace: Building Organizational Cultures That Thrive," Gallup, https://www.gallup.com/analytics/472658/workplace-recognition-research.aspx#:~:text=45%25%20Well%2Drecognized%20employees%20are,as%20likely%20to%20be%20engaged.

xxxviii *Ibid.*

xxxix Peter M. Blau, *Exchange and Power in Social Life* (New York: John Wiley & Sons, 1964).

xl   *Ibid.*